THE ANCIENT GREEK WORLD

**RONALD MELLOR &
AMANDA H. PODANY**
GENERAL EDITORS

THE ANCIENT
GREEK WORLD

Jennifer T. Roberts & Tracy Barrett

OXFORD
UNIVERSITY PRESS

For R. Ross Holloway, who first opened my eyes
to the beauty of Greek art —T. B.

For my grandchildren —J. R.

OXFORD
UNIVERSITY PRESS

Oxford   New York

Auckland   Bangkok   Buenos Aires   Cape Town   Chennai   Dar es Salaam   Delhi   Hong Kong   Istanbul
Karachi   Kolkata   Kuala Lumpur   Madrid   Melbourne   Mexico City   Mumbai   Nairobi   São Paulo
Shanghai   Singapore   Taipei   Tokyo   Toronto

Published by Oxford University Press, Inc.
198 Madison Avenue, New York, New York 10016
www.oup.com

Library of Congress Cataloging-in-Publication Data

Roberts, Jennifer T.
  The ancient Greek world / Jennifer T. Roberts & Tracy Barrett.
     p. cm. — (The world in ancient times)
Summary: Introduces the history, culture, and people of ancient Greece
and examines its many contributions to the development of Western society.
  ISBN 0-19-515696-X (alk. paper)
  1. Greece—History—To 146 B.C.—Juvenile literature. 2.
Greece—History—To 146 B.C.—Sources—Juvenile literature. [1.
Greece—History—To 146 B.C. 2. Greece—Civilization—To 146 B.C.] I.
Barrett, Tracy, II. Title. III. Series.
  DF215 .R633 2004
  938—dc22
                              2003017875
9 8 7 6 5 4 3 2 1

Printed in Hong Kong on acid-free paper

Design: Stephanie Blumenthal
Layout: Alexis Siroc and Lenny Levitsky
Cover design and logo: Nora Wertz

On the cover: Over the centuries, some of the paint and facial features have worn off of this painted Greek mask.
Frontispiece: In this scene on a stone coffin from the late fourth century BCE, Alexander joins some
Persians in a lion hunt.

RONALD MELLOR &
AMANDA H. PODANY
GENERAL EDITORS

The Early Human World
Peter Robertshaw & Jill Rubalcaba

The Ancient Near Eastern World
Amanda H. Podany & Marni McGee

The Ancient Egyptian World
Eric H. Cline & Jill Rubalcaba

The Ancient South Asian World
Jonathan Mark Kenoyer & Kimberley Heuston

The Ancient Chinese World
Terry Kleeman & Tracy Barrett

The Ancient Greek World
Jennifer T. Roberts & Tracy Barrett

The Ancient Roman World
Ronald Mellor & Marni McGee

The Ancient American World
William Fash & Mary E. Lyons

CONTENTS

*A 〔"〕 marks each chapter's primary sources—ancient writings
and artifacts that "speak" to us from the past.*

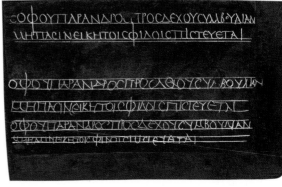

CAST OF CHARACTERS

Because The World in Ancient Times *covers many cultures, we use the abbreviations CE for "Common Era" and BCE for "Before the Common Era." The traditional equivalents are BC for "Before Christ" and AD for "Anno Domini," Latin for "In the Year of Our Lord," referring to the birth of Jesus Christ.*

Achilles (uh-KIL-eez) Mythical Greek warrior in the Trojan War

Aeschylus (ES-kuh-lus), about 525–456 BCE Athenian playwright

Aesop (EE-sop), sixth century BCE Greek slave and storyteller

Agamemnon (AG-uh-MEM-non) Mythical king of Mycenae

Alcibiades (AL-suh-BY-uh-deez), about 450–404 BCE Athenian general and politician

Alexander, 356–323 BCE King of Macedon (ruled 336–323 BCE); son of Philip of Macedon

Antigone (an-TIG-uh-nee) Mythical daughter of Oedipus

Aphrodite (AF-ruh-DIE-tee) Mythical goddess of love

Apollo (uh-PA-low) Mythical god of the sun, archery, and prophecy

Archimedes (AHR-kuh-ME-deez), about 285–212 BCE Mathematician and engineer; developed system of measuring area and volume

Ares (EHR-eez) Mythical god of war

Aristagoras (ar-i-STAG-uh-rus), fifth century BCE Tyrant of the *polis* of Miletus

Aristides (ar-i-STEE-deez), fifth century BCE Athenian statesman and general; helped to found the Delian League

Aristophanes (ar-i-STAHF-uh-neez), about 450–388 BCE Athenian playwright who wrote comedies

Aristotle (ar-i-STAH-tl), 384–322 BCE Philosopher and teacher; founded the Lyceum

Artemis (AHR-ti-mus) Mythical goddess of hunting and the moon

Artemisia (AHR-ti-MIZ-ee-uh), fifth century BCE Queen of Halicarnassus

Athena (uh-THEE-nuh) Mythical goddess of war and wisdom, patron deity of Athens

Athenaeus (ATH-i-NEE-us), about 200 CE Writer who wrote about banquets and food

Bacchylides (buh-KIL-i-deez), fifth century BCE Poet who wrote about the Olympic games

Callimachus (kuh-LIM-uh-kus), about 305–240 BCE Poet who wrote during the Hellenistic period

Cleomenes (klee-AH-muh-neez), about 520–490 BCE King of Sparta

Clytemnestra (KLIE-tim-NES-truh) Mythical wife of King Agamemnon

Creon (KREE-ahn) Mythical king in Sophocles' play *Antigone*

Cronos (KROH-nus) Mythical king of Titans

Daedalus (DED-l-us) Mythical architect who made wings out of birds' feathers and wax

Darius (duh-RYE-us) 550–486 BCE Persian emperor (ruled 521–486 BCE); he fought the Greeks after the revolt of the Ionians

Demeter (di-ME-ter) Mythical goddess of the harvest

Democritus (di-MOK-ruh-tus), about 460–370 BCE Philosopher and scientist; he theorized the world is made up of atoms

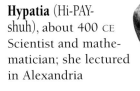

Demosthenes (di-MOSS-thuh-neez), 384–322 BCE   Athenian orator

Diodorus Siculus (die-uh-DAWR-us SIK-yuh-lus), first century BCE   Historian; he wrote *Library of History*

Dionysius (DIE-un-EYE-shus) **I**, about 430–367 BCE   Tyrant of Syracuse

Dionysus (DIE-un-EYE-sus)   Mythical god of wine

Eratosthenes (EHR-uh-TAHS-thuh-neez), about 276–194 BCE   Scientist who calculated the earth's size

Eros (EHR-oas)   Mythical god of love

Euripides (yoo-RIP-i-deez), about 484–406 BCE   Playwright; he wrote *Iphigenia Among the Taurians* and *The Trojan Women*

Evans, Sir Arthur, 1851–1941   Archaeologist; he excavated the palace of Knossos

Gorgo (GAWR-goh), fifth century BCE   Daughter of King Cleomenes of Sparta who married King Leonidas

Hades (HAY-deez)   Mythical lord of the underworld

Haemon (HE-mun)   Mythical son of King Creon

Hector   Mythical Trojan prince who fought in the Trojan War

Helen of Troy   Character in Greek mythology viewed as the most beautiful woman in the world and the cause of the Trojan War

Hera (HAIR-uh)   Mythical queen of the gods

Heracles (HAIR-uh-kleez)   Mythical demigod, son of Zeus and a mortal, known for superhuman strength and cunning

Hermes (HER-meez)   Mythical messenger of the gods, who carried caduceus

Herodotus (huh-RAH-duh-tus), about 484–420 BCE   Historian who wrote his *Histories* about the Persian wars

Hesiod (HE-see-ud), about 700 BCE   Early poet

Hippocrates (hi-PAHK-ruh-teez), fifth century BCE   Physician who believed there is reason for illness; credited with the Hippocratic Oath.

Homer, eighth century BCE   Epic poet; he wrote the *Iliad* and the *Odyssey*

Hypatia (Hi-PAY-shuh), about 400 CE   Scientist and mathematician; she lectured in Alexandria

Isocrates (eye-SAHK-ruh-teez), 436–338 BCE   Athenian statesman who wrote the *Antidosis*

Leonidas (lee-AHN-i-dus)   King of Sparta (ruled 490–480 BCE) who died fighting at Thermopylae

Lycurgus (lie-KUHR-gus), seventh century BCE   Spartan lawgiver; he was credited with establishing the Spartans' war-centered life

Minos (MY-nus)   Mythical king of Minoans whose son the minotaur was kept in a labyrinth below the king's palace

Odysseus (oh-DIS-ee-us)   Mythical Greek hero of Homer's *Odyssey*

Olympias (uh-LIM-pee-us), about 375–316 BCE   Wife of Philip of Macedon

Paris   Mythical Trojan prince who agreed to give a golden apple to Aphrodite in exchange for Helen

Pasion (PAHZ-ee-ohn), fourth century BCE   Former slave at Athens who became a wealthy banker

Pausanias (paw-SAY-nee-us), d. 336 BCE   Assassinated King Philip of Macedon

Pausanias (paw-SAY-nee-us), second century CE   Travel writer; he wrote *Description of Greece*

Peisistratus (pi-SIS-truh-tus), sixth century BCE Athenian tyrant who increased trade, minted coins, and encouraged arts in pottery and vase painting

Penelope (puh-NEL-uh-pee) Mythical wife of Odysseus

Pericles (PAIR-i-kleez), about 495–429 BCE Athenian statesman who reformed laws to give lower classes more power for a more democratic society

Pheidias (FID-ee-us), fifth century BCE Sculptor

Philip of Macedon (MASS-i-don), King of Macedon (ruled 359–336 BCE) and conqueror of Greece

Phintys (FIN-tis), about 200 BCE Writer; she wrote about differences between men and women

Plato (PLAY-toh), about 427–347 BCE Philosopher and teacher who founded the Academy and wrote the *Republic*

Plutarch (PLOO-tark), 46–after 119 CE Biographer and essayist who wrote in Roman times

Polykleitos (PAH-li-KLIE-tus), 460–410 BCE Sculptor

Polyphemus (PA-li-FEE-mus) Cyclops, mythical figure, who imprisoned Odysseus and his sailors in Homer's *Odyssey*

Poseidon (puh-SIDE-un) Mythical god of ocean and earthquakes

Protagoras (proh-TAG-uh-rus), about 485–410 BCE Philosopher and Sophist; he said "Man is the measure of all things"

Ptolemy (TAL-uh-mee), 323–285 BCE General under Alexander; governor and later ruler of Egypt; he built the Mouseion and Library at Alexandria

Pythagoras (pi-THAG-uh-rus), about 580–500 BCE Mathematician who discovered the Pythagorean theorem

Sappho (SAF-oh), seventh to sixth century BCE Poet who was so admired by her contemporaries that she was sometimes called "the tenth muse"

Schliemann (SHLEE-mahn), **Heinrich**, (HINE-rikh), 1822–1890 Archaeologist who claimed to have found the site of ancient Troy

Semonides (se-MAH-ni-deez), about 650 BCE Poet who wrote satire comparing women to animals

Simonides (see-MAH-ni-deez), about 556–468 BCE Poet

Socrates (SOCK-ruh-teez), about 470–399 BCE Philosopher who invented a question-and-answer format called the Socratic method

Solon (SOH-lun), about 630–560 BCE Athenian poet, politician, and lawgiver who is known as one of the "Seven Wise Men of Greece"

Sophocles (SAW-fuh-kleez), about 524–406 BCE Playwright who wrote Greek tragedies including *Antigone* and *Oedipus*

Themistocles (thuh-MIS-tuh-kleez), about 524–460 BCE Athenian politician and general

Theseus (THEE-see-us) Mythical Athenian prince who killed the Minotaur

Thucydides (thoo-SID-i-deez), about 460–after 404 BCE Historian; he wrote *The History of the Peloponnesian War*

Tyrtaeus (tur-TEE-us), seventh century BCE Spartan poet

Ventris, **Michael**, 1922–1956 English architect who deciphered Linear B tablets

Xenophon (ZEN-uh-fun), 431–after 350 BCE Historian

Xerxes (ZURK-seez), 486–465 BCE King of Persia who defeated the Spartans led by Leonidas at Thermopylae

Zeus (zoose) Mythical son of Cronos and chief god of the Greeks

GREEK SETTLEMENTS AT THE DEATH OF ALEXANDER THE GREAT
323 BCE

Caspian Sea

Tigris River

Persian Gulf

AFGHANISTAN

PAKISTAN

Indus River

INDIA

ARABIA

Indian Ocean

| 0 | | 400 mi |
| 0 | | 600 km |

SOME PRONUNCIATIONS

Akragas (uh-KRAH-gus)
Anatolia (an-uh-TOE-lee-uh)
Antioch (AHN-tee-ock)
Babylon (BA-buh-lun)
Carthage (KAHR-thij)
Crete (kreet)
Cyrene (sigh-REE-nee)
Damascus (duh-MASS-cus)
Euphrates (yoo-FRAY-teez) River
Gades (KAY-deez)
Indus (IN-dus) River
Knossos (NAHS-us)
Massilia (mass-SILL-ee-uh)
Neapolis (nee-A-puh-lis)
Sybaris (SEE-buh-rus)
Syracuse (SEER-uh-kyoos)

INTRODUCTION
THE GLORY THAT WAS GREECE

*philos + sophia =
"love" + "wisdom"
Originally, "philosophy"
meant "love of wisdom," but
now it means a set of beliefs
or the study of the truth.
A philosopher searches for
meaning in life: some by
studying ethics, others by
studying the nature of reality.*

The ancient Greeks came up with some of the most interesting ideas, the most beautiful art, the greatest stories,
and the most magnificent cities and buildings that the world
has ever known. They introduced democracy. Their
philosophers taught people new ways of thinking. Their
ships revolutionized sea travel and opened up trade and
exploration. Their art and architecture have inspired artists
for thousands of years. Many countries today have democracies like those invented in Greece, and Greek plays are still
performed in different languages all over the world. Many
modern buildings are modeled on Greek temples.

That's not to say that Greek society was perfect. The reason the philosophers and poets were able to think beautiful
thoughts was that they didn't have to spend their time
doing hard work. Instead, slaves, poorly paid servants, and
overworked laborers did most of the dangerous or difficult
jobs. Hundreds of thousands of people who lived in Greece
were enslaved. In fact, one reason people fought hard in war
was that they knew that the losers often became slaves of
the winners.

*Every two years, women walked to
the mountains to perform religious
rituals to honor the god Dionysus
with dances and music. On this
stone coffin, worshipers (center) are
dancing with satyrs, mythological
creatures that were supposed to be
half goat, half human.*

Aside from enslaving people, the Greeks waged many wars that might strike people of today as unjustified. They were sometimes prejudiced, looking down on non-Greek people. Women weren't allowed anything close to the same rights and freedom as men.

Still, the Greeks achieved extraordinary things. And they knew they were special. Early on, they started writing about themselves. They were the first people in the ancient western world to write what we now call history: a narrative of what happened to the people, and what the people did. Other ancient peoples centered their histories around the gods or around their ruler.

One of the earliest Greek historians, Herodotus, lived in the fifth century BCE. He was eager for future generations to remember the great things his own people and the other peoples living nearby did. So he says at the beginning of his *Histories*,

Herodotus's hometown was Halicarnassus, a Greek city under Persian control.

This is where Herodotus of Halicarnassus has set forth the fruits of his research, a project he undertook so that the great and wonderful achievements of both Greeks and **barbarians** should not go unrenowned.

❝ Herodotus, *Histories*, mid-fifth century BCE

"Barbarian" comes from *barbaros*, which means "a foreigner."

Another great Greek historian, Thucydides, also thought it was important for others to appreciate his people's greatness, and wrote in *The History of the Peloponnesian War*:

I, Thucydides of Athens, wrote the history of the war that was fought between the Spartans and the Athenians. I began the history as soon as the war broke out, in the belief that it would be the most important, most interesting war of any that had gone before. . . . This was the greatest movement ever to sweep the Greeks and many of the barbarians—in other words, the majority of the human race.

❝ Thucydides, *The History of the Peloponnesian War*, 431 BCE

But Thucydides had another reason for writing history. He was sure that he could do it better than anyone else, and would get the facts straight. He was distressed that people

The Greek historian Thucydides wrote The History of the Peloponnesian War *so that people could learn history from facts, rather than from myths and legends.*

"Hero" comes from *heros*, which means "a man of unusual strength, courage, or ability."

seemed to be more interested in exciting stories and tales of **heroes** than in what really happened.

Thucydides was right to worry that people might look to myths and legends to find out about the past. This has happened for a long time, and still goes on today. People can get so caught up in a myth that they believe that it tells the "real story."

And it's true that some myths are loosely based on real events. The Trojan War, or something like it, might really have happened. It's possible that people made up stories about centaurs—half man, half horse—the first time they saw someone on a horse.

But most Greek myths aren't history. Instead, they are stories that teach a lesson, or give an explanation for why something exists in a certain way in nature, or just entertain and amuse an audience. The Greeks were master storytellers, and the tales of their gods and goddesses, their nymphs and satyrs, and their interactions with human beings have lasted for millennia. Even if the Greeks had not given us anything else, their myths and legends are enough to make us appreciate their creativity and imagination.

Some centaurs got drunk and tried to kidnap women attending a wedding. Sculptures of the battle that erupted between these unruly guests and their hosts filled spaces on the outside wall of the Parthenon in Athens.

CHAPTER 1

WHAT'S A GREEK?
GREECE AND GREEKS

Where is Greece? Who are the Greek people? Nowadays, it's easy to answer these questions. Any encyclopedia or atlas shows where Greece is, what borders define it, and which islands in the Mediterranean Sea are Greek and which are part of Turkey or Italy or someplace else. And it's easy enough to say who the Greek people are—they are the citizens of Greece.

But it would have been hard to answer those questions 2,500 years ago. At that time there was no such country as "Greece," and the people who lived in what we now call "Greece" didn't consider that they all lived in the same country. They lived in communities that governed themselves without consulting each other. Sometimes they were at war with each other and sometimes they formed alliances, but they were separate and independent.

And if there was no such country as Greece, who were the Greeks?

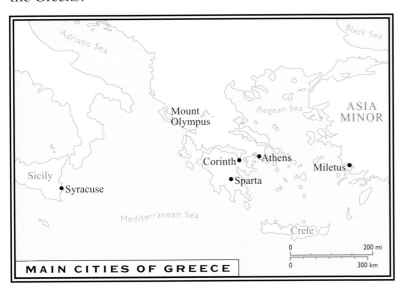

MAIN CITIES OF GREECE

Basically, when we say the "the ancient Greeks," we mean the people who lived near the Mediterranean Sea between about 2000 BCE and 500 CE and who spoke Greek, a member of the family of languages that we now call Indo-European. But since it takes too long to write "the people who spoke Greek," from now on we'll just call them "the Greeks."

The Greeks had more than just their Indo-European heritage and their language in common. They also shared many traditions and customs. They sometimes got together for sporting events and other festivals.

It's difficult to go further than that, or even to define where exactly the Greeks lived, since they traveled and set up colonies in what are now other countries. Some of these colonies lasted for centuries, but some were unsuccessful and the Greeks in them died or came home in a short time.

One other element that united the Greeks was their religion.

In the northern part of what is now Greece stands a mountain so high (9,573 feet, or 2,918 meters) that visitors often can't see the top of it through the mist that cloaks its sides. The beautiful Mount Olympus looks mysterious, and a modern tourist driving past can easily see why the Greeks thought that something special must be at its peak. They thought that the top of the mountain was the home of their gods.

The Greeks believed that gods walked the earth along with people. They were different from people in that they could never die and they had magical powers. But they also loved and hated, got angry, made peace, and performed kind deeds and some foolish ones—behaved a lot like human beings, in fact. And just like humans, they had to live someplace. What could be a better home for them than a mountain that stretched so high that it seemed to be a halfway point between the heavens and the earth?

If the Greek gods decided to use their extra-sharp eyes to look over the whole area filled with people who believed in and worshiped them, what would they see?

They would see a large body of water with many islands, some so tiny that a person could easily swim around them,

Sure-footed goats were well adapted for life in rocky Greece. Their milk, wool, meat, and hides were useful products, and their strong little bodies could carry people and other burdens. This pelike *was a kind of pot used for holding wine or water.*

The Greek World

The philosopher Plato realized that the people who spoke Greek took up only a small part of the land around them. He wrote in his dialogue the *Phaedo,*

"*T*he earth, if you ask me, is quite vast, and those of us who live between the Pillars of Heracles and the river Phasis [the then-known world] inhabit only a small part of it around the sea, like ants or frogs around a pond."

and some so large that it would take days to walk across them. They would see lands curving into and out of this sea, with mountains that had been formed by volcanoes. The land that was the home of the people who called themselves "Hellenes," and whom we now call "the ancient Greeks," originally was a small area bordering the Aegean Sea and some islands near that land. Eventually the Greeks occupied territory that stretched from Spain in the west to what is now Turkey, and eventually even India in the east.

The land explains a lot about the Greeks and their way of life. The mountains aren't particularly high, but they cover four-fifths of the Greek mainland. This is one reason why the Greeks didn't feel united with each other. In the earliest days of Greek civilization, there weren't even any horses. It took days or weeks to get from one area to another on foot, so it would have been difficult to feel like a fellow citizen with someone from a different place. Messengers would take a long time to carry word from one place to another and could get lost or even killed on their way, so communication was slow and uncertain.

The mountains defined other things about the Greeks. For example, olives and grapes grow well on their slopes, but wheat and other grains need a different kind of soil and flatter land for plowing. Sheep, goats, and pigs can thrive in areas that are too steep for cows and other large animals. It's

Whole families joined in the grape harvest. The artist who decorated this vase emphasized the graceful curves of a grapevine.

not surprising, then, that the Greeks grew olives and grapes and raised many of these smaller animals. Cows belonged mostly to wealthy people, and for a long time wheat had to be imported.

Life by the sea molded the Greek character and Greek society. The warm water kept the winters from being very cold, and the Greeks spent much of their time outdoors. They shopped in open-air markets and conducted much of their legal business out in public where everyone could see it. Plays were held in outdoor theaters, and elections were held outside on a hill called the Pnyx.

The sea helped the Greeks' economy, too. They had to travel to trade their precious olive oil and wine for other supplies such as wood, metal ores, grain, and animal products like meat, hides, and wool. So they developed fast, sturdy boats and learned how to navigate.

The sailors didn't just trade. Some of them became pirates, and travelers also would take advantage of any opportunity to conquer other people and take their belongings. In the epic poem the *Odyssey*, written about 725 BCE, the Greek hero Odysseus spent many years sailing home from war. Whenever he had the chance to raid the cities he came across on his travels, he did so. The author of the *Odyssey*, Homer, says that Odysseus boasted to one king he met on his journey,

❝ Homer, *Odyssey*, about 725 BCE

From Troy, the great winds seized us and then let us off
At Ismarus . . .
I sacked the city and I killed its folk,
And taking all the women and the goods,
We split them up amongst ourselves, fairly,
In such a way that none would get shortchanged.

Apparently, it didn't occur to Odysseus that the women of Ismarus were also people, and that the "folk" whose possessions got split up evenly among the raiders would disagree with his idea of what's fair and what isn't.

Some other ancient people were afraid of the Greeks because of their skill at seafaring and their piracy. In the *Odyssey*, the mythical cyclops Polyphemus spoke for a lot of the neighbors of the Greeks when he asks Odysseus,

> Strangers, who are you?
> From where do you come sailing o'er the watery way?
> Is it on some business, or are you recklessly roving
> As pirates do, when they sail on the salt sea and venture
> Their lives as they wander, bringing evil to alien people?

❝ Homer, *Odyssey*, about 725 BCE

So the land and sea shaped the Greeks. But the Greeks were curious and inventive people, and they took what nature had given them as a starting point for new achievements. In time their gods were able to look down from Mount Olympus onto amazing cities. The goddess Athena could see workmen bustling around her special city, Athens, building the temple to her called the Parthenon. The king of the gods, Zeus, had a great seat from which to watch the games that were held in his honor every four years, many miles away. All the gods could observe people gather together and vote, watch plays, or argue over important questions. The civilization the Greeks were carving out in this beautiful land was something that the world had never seen before, and that still influences our lives today.

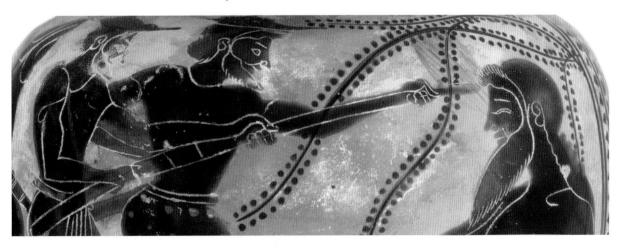

The giant cyclops Polyphemus (here shrunk down to fit on a pot) was blinded by Odysseus and his men after he started eating their companions.

CHAPTER 2

GODS, PRIESTS, AND ORACLES
GREEK RELIGION

All families have their ups and downs, but one family in particular had more than its share of both. A father who ate his children, siblings who couldn't get along and had to live on opposite ends of the world, husbands and wives who constantly cheated on each other—a nasty bunch.

They did have some good things going for them, though, including eternal life and people so eager to make them happy that they gave them precious objects. Those same people built beautiful temples to the members of this family and made such tall and handsome statues of them that others came from miles around just to see them. A little family discord might seem a small price to pay.

This family was, of course, not a normal one, but the family of the Greek gods, who lived on Mount Olympus (or

The temple of Poseidon at Cape Sounion has long been a favorite spot for tourists. The English poet Lord Byron visited it in the 1800s and carved his name on a column.

at least that's what the ancient Greeks believed). They were also perfectly at home on the earth. For the ancient Greeks, the gods were all around, and if you never happened to see one, maybe you would some other day.

The Greek gods were very much like humans in many ways. They ate and drank, they fell in love, they had children, they got into trouble, they had wars—they did everything people did (except die), only on a much larger scale.

So who were they? And where did they come from?

The Greeks thought that once the whole universe was a big swirling nothingness called Chaos. Suddenly a black-winged bird appeared and laid an egg. The egg cracked open, and Eros, the god of love, was born. The top half of the egg flew upward and became Uranus, the sky. The bottom half fell and turned into Gaea, the earth.

Rhea holds a rock, dressed in baby clothes, out to Cronos, hoping he will be fooled into thinking it is baby Zeus. This krater, *or vase, was made in the fifth century* BCE.

Uranus and Gaea fell in love. It's not like they had much choice! There wasn't anyone else there except Eros, and having the god of love flying around might have helped. They had lots of children, called the Titans.

One of their children, Cronos, had a particularly nasty disposition. In fact, he was so worried that one of his children would replace him as the top Titan that as soon as his wife had a baby, he would eat it.

For a while his wife went along with this. But she got sick of seeing her babies disappear into her husband's huge mouth. So when she had her sixth child, a little boy she named Zeus, she wrapped up a stone in baby clothes and gave it to Cronos. He must not have been too bright because he swallowed it and never noticed that it wasn't his son.

After baby Zeus grew up, his father vomited up the other five children: his sons Hades and Poseidon and their sisters Hera, Demeter, and Hestia. It turns out that they were immortal, so instead

THE 12 GREEK GODS AND THEIR MAIN FUNCTIONS

Zeus	*king of the gods and lord of the sky*
Hera	*queen of the gods*
Poseidon	*lord of the oceans and earthquakes*
Hades	*lord of the underworld*
Hephaestus	*god of metal-working*
Aphrodite	*goddess of love*
Ares	*god of war*
Athena	*goddess of war and wisdom*
Apollo	*god of the arts and the sun*
Artemis	*goddess of hunting and the moon*
Hermes	*messenger of the gods*
Dionysus	*god of wine*

a + mbrosis = "not" + "having to do with mortals" When people say that a food is like ambrosia, they mean it is delicious or "fit for the gods" who were immortal.

of dying when they were eaten, they had survived. They grew during their wait and emerged as adults. Cronos was so terrified at the sight of his strong children that he ran away.

The six children of Cronos moved to Mount Olympus. In time some of their children joined them, and eventually 12 deities (gods and goddesses) were seated on thrones in the palace on the mountain. Hades and Poseidon didn't get along well with each other or with their brother Zeus, and they spent most of their time in their own faraway kingdoms: Hades ruled the underworld and Poseidon was the lord of the sea.

The gods lived on their mountain, eating a special food called **ambrosia** and drinking nectar. But they also went down to earth from time to time to see what was going on with the humans who worshiped them.

They didn't just watch, however. They got involved with life on earth. They had a tendency to fall in love with humans. This was a problem, because not only did the gods live forever, but they never got old, either. So it was sad for them to see the person they were in love with grow wrinkled and sick and eventually die, while they themselves remained as young and beautiful as ever.

Still, that didn't stop them from falling in love. Zeus in particular had many children whose mothers were human. Some of the children of these mixed marriages were mortal, but some became gods. The twins Artemis and Apollo, for example, had a human mother named Leto. Zeus's wife Hera was so furious when she found out that Leto was pregnant that she prohibited all the lands from giving Leto a resting place where she could give birth. Leto wandered until she found a little island named Delos that was so new that it was still floating instead of being attached to the ocean bottom. (New islands don't really float, but the Greeks didn't know that.) Since it wasn't technically part of the land, it didn't have to follow Hera's orders, so Leto could rest there long enough to have her twins.

Sometimes the gods were nice to humans. A kind old couple once took in some travelers, and even though they were poor, they gave the travelers a good dinner. They were astonished when their pitchers and serving dishes kept magically refilling, no matter how many servings were taken from them. It turned out that the two visitors were the gods Hermes and Zeus. They were so pleased at the way the old couple had treated them that they granted the old couple one wish. They were so much in love that they asked the favor of dying at the same time, since neither one would want to live without the other. The gods gladly granted

The 17th-century Italian artist Gian Lorenzo Bernini's statue Apollo and Daphne *tells their story. When the beautiful nymph Daphne ran away from Apollo, he chased after her. She prayed for help and turned into a laurel tree. Apollo was so sad that he adopted the laurel as one of his special symbols.*

Hymn to Poseidon

Many ancient people thought that earthquakes were caused by the motion of the sea on the earth, or water leaking into cracks in the land. This is why Poseidon, god of the sea, was also god of earthquakes.

"I begin to sing of the great god Poseidon, mover of the earth and of the barren sea. . . . The gods gave you a double assignment, O Earth-Shaker: to be a tamer of horses and a savior of ships. Hail Poseidon, Holder of the Earth, Dark-haired Lord! O blessed one, be kind in your heart, and helpful to those who make ocean voyages!"

Homer, *Iliad*, about 750 BCE

this request. Years later, when they were too old to go on living, they both turned into trees that grew with their branches intertwined.

So at any time, any passing stranger could be a god. It paid to be nice to people, just in case.

It stood to reason that if the gods were similar to humans, the things that people like would make the gods happy, too. Most people like to be told how great they are, so making up nice songs and poems about how beautiful and strong and wise the gods were would make them like the person who wrote or performed them.

People also like to get presents. So it would help to leave gifts in the temples, and burn meat so that the smoke would rise to Mount Olympus and the gods could feast on it. (Although they ate nothing but ambrosia, they liked the smell of cooked food, and it nourished them.)

Some people served as priests, dedicating their lives to serving the gods, usually choosing one god in particular. In a temple on Delos, the priests made sacrifices to Apollo and Artemis. On Cape Sounion, a cliff overlooking the sea, a gleaming white temple to Poseidon served both as a place for the priests to worship the sea-god and as a kind of lighthouse. When sailors caught sight of it, they knew they were getting close to home and would thank Poseidon for giving them a safe journey. Once, when a priest of Apollo wanted a favor from the god, he reminded Apollo of all his sacrifices. Homer reports the priest's words in the *Iliad*:

> If ever it pleased your heart that I built your temple,
> If ever it pleased you that I burnt all the rich thigh pieces
> Of bulls, of goats, then bring to pass this wish I pray for.

Apollo must have felt he owed the priest a favor because he granted the priest's prayer.

So the priests helped the people by being in charge of the temples and the sacrifices. They also predicted what was going to happen. Birds flying in a certain direction, for example, meant good luck. An animal born deformed meant bad luck. But sometimes it was hard to know what the gods wanted. To find out, people turned to the oracles.

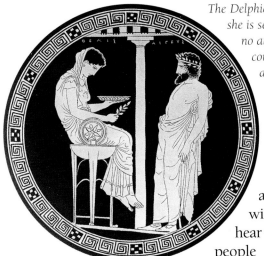

The Delphic sibyl is so absorbed in what she is seeing in her dish that she pays no attention to the king who has come to consult her. She clutches a laurel branch, the symbol of the god Apollo, who was worshiped at Delphi.

An oracle was a place that had a special connection with a god, and was also the person connected with that place who could hear what the god said. These people were more often called prophets or sibyls. Prophets were often ordinary people, not priests. Sometimes they thought they could hear what a god said and reported it to the people, but more often, they went into a kind of trance and start talking in the voice of the god. When they came out of the trance, they often had no idea of what they had been saying and had to ask the people around them what the god wanted. Oracles were just like stereo speakers; they had no control over what sound went through them.

Sometimes it was hard to understand what the oracle was saying. The oracle at Cumae, in a part of Italy settled by Greeks, wrote her prophecies on leaves. She lived in a room at the end of a long tunnel carved into the side of a hill. When a person seeking an answer opened the door to her room, the wind made the leaves swirl around. The person had to put the leaves back together and hope they got them in the right order. Other times, an oracle said something that could be interpreted in different ways. One told a king that if he went to battle, there would be a great victory. Later, when the defeated monarch returned to remind her of what she had predicted, the oracle said, "There *was* a great victory—it just didn't happen to be yours!"

So dealing with the gods was sometimes frustrating. But the Greeks expected this. Life is often unfair, and the gods were part of life.

THE DELPHIC SIBYL

The most famous Greek oracle was in Delphi. After a ritual of chewing laurel leaves, bathing, and other activities, the prophet sat on a special three-legged stool. After a while she appeared to go into a trance, and then started talking, often making little or no sense. A priest had to tell people what she meant.

In 2002, a team of scientists discovered a rock under the floor of the temple of Apollo at Delphi that when rubbed produces sweet gas. Small amounts of it can make people feel separated from the real world. There are frequently small earthquakes in Greece, which might have produced enough of this gas to make the oracle feel she was channeling the god.

CHAPTER 3

MYSTERIOUS MINOANS
THE EARLIEST GREEKS

❝ The Palace of Knossos at Crete,
about 1450 BCE

*This huge structure spans 5.5 acres
and is called the palace of Knossos,
although scholars disagree about what
its main purpose was.*

S ome of the early people who lived in the area that is now
Greece weren't actually Greek. They were people we
now call Minoans.

The Minoans appeared on the island of Crete about
8,000 years ago. They raised sheep and goats and grew
wheat, none of which was found on Crete before the
Minoans arrived. So we can figure that they probably came
from someplace in the Near East, where farmers had been

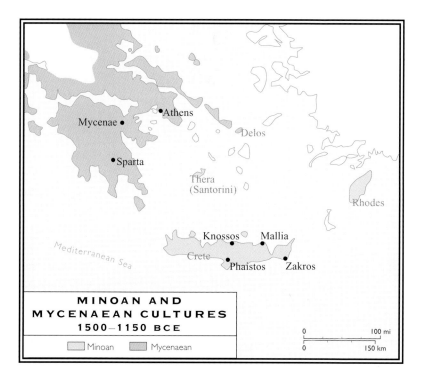

MINOAN AND
MYCENAEAN CULTURES
1500–1150 BCE

Minoan   Mycenaean

0   100 mi
0   150 km

raising sheep and goats and growing wheat for some time, and that they brought animals and seeds with them.

The Minoan villages grew into cities, and their civilization became strong. In the third millenium BCE, they started building palaces. The palaces were probably originally built to store valuable grain and to house powerful people. Many of the palaces were destroyed in some huge **catastrophe**—probably an earthquake around 1700 BCE, although nobody knows for sure.

When the palaces were rebuilt, they were even more splendid and complex than they had been before the disaster. The most beautiful palace was in the city of Knossos, near Crete's northern shore.

The Minoans were great sailors and traders. They developed a written language and had a religion that might have included worship of both a fertility goddess and a bull-god. At some point in the second millennium BCE, they suffered two disasters: a flood and a huge fire, and their civilization never recovered.

kata + *strophe* = "down" + "turn." "Catastrophe" originally meant "an overturning," like knocking something over so that everything spills out. Later it came to mean a turning point, such as the part of a story when everything changes. Now it means "a disaster."

These crude-looking marks, formed by scratching in wet clay, are in Linear A, a script used by Minoans. Unfortunately, nobody has deciphered the script to know what the markings mean.

Unfortunately, we don't know a lot about this strong and important civilization. The main problem is that we can't read their language, which we call Linear A ("linear" because it is written in a straight line, and "A" because it is earlier than the other script, called "Linear B").

Here are some of the mysteries about the Minoans:

- Where exactly did they come from, and why did they go to Crete?
- What kind of government did they have? Most civilizations in that area at the time were ruled by a king, but it's possible that the Minoans were different. They might have had a council of nobles.
- What did they trade with other countries? They had to have had something valuable, since what they got in exchange were expensive luxury items like metals and ivory.
- How much influence did other civilizations have on them? Egypt was so powerful at this time that Egypt and the Minoans must have worked together sometimes and traded with each other.
- Were men and women treated about the same? That would be very unusual, but the artwork shows both sexes together and doing about the same things. On the other hand, people often show things in art that don't happen in real life.
- Those buildings we call "palaces"—what were they used for? People usually assume they were the homes of the kings. But we don't even know if there were kings in Crete. The palaces look more like huge storage buildings for grain. Why would they need to store so much grain?
- What destroyed the palaces around 1450 BCE?

The Greeks who came after the Minoans were as interested in them as we are. They said that the Minoans' most well-known king was a powerful man named Minos. He was incredibly rich, and a judge and lawgiver. The poet Homer called him "companion of mighty Zeus." The historian

Thucydides was convinced that Minos was a great military leader. He wrote in *The History of the Peloponnesian War* that

> Greeks have learned from their parents that Minos was the earliest man to build a navy, and he controlled most of what is now the Aegean Sea. He also ruled the Cyclades Islands and was the first to colonize most of the [nearby] islands, and he set up his own sons in power. It is likely that he did this to get rid of pirates so that they wouldn't interfere with his making money by trading.

Minos had one problem, though. He had a monstrous son (or perhaps stepson) who was half human and half bull. The two words "Minos" and *tauros* ("bull") make up the name of this monster: the Minotaur. He was so ferocious that he ate only human flesh. It's unclear why Minos kept him alive. Maybe he was fond of the Minotaur even though he was a monster. Maybe he was afraid that he would get in trouble if he killed him—a half human, half bull must have some connection with the gods, after all.

Minos kept the monster under the palace in a big maze called the labyrinth. Minos ordered the Athenians (his enemies) to send him their own children so the monster would have enough to eat. Minos was so powerful that the Athenians obeyed for a long time.

Finally, an Athenian prince named Theseus made up his mind that he was going to put an end to this slaughter. Luckily for the prince, he didn't have to work alone. Minos's daughter Ariadne fell in love with him. She gave him a sword and a ball of yarn and told him to unwind it behind him as he went to the center of the labyrinth where the Minotaur lived. When he had killed the Minotaur, all he had to do was follow the yarn back out.

It worked. The Minotaur was killed, and Ariadne ran away with Theseus. (He left her for another woman almost right away, but that's another story.)

Who would ever believe such a weird tale? Oddly enough, many people. Some people in recent times have thought that some of it might be based on fact. There certainly was

66 Thucydides, *The History of the Peloponnesian War*, 431 BCE

A SWEET SOLUTION

According to mythology, the labyrinth where Minos kept the Minotaur was constructed by Daedalus, a great architect. Among his feats was learning how to fly by making wings out of birds' feathers and wax. Daedalus figured out how to get a thread up the winding passages of a seashell and out a hole bored in the top.

His solution was to tie the thread (which must have been very, very thin) to the leg of an ant (which must have been very, very large). He put a drop of honey at the hole in the top of the shell and the ant at the opening at the bottom. The ant, attracted by the sweet smell, walked through the whole shell, around all its turns, dragging the thread behind, and came out at the other end.

Some people, including Sir Arthur Evans, have thought the center chair—with its graceful carvings and the high back—was a throne. But there is no evidence to support that theory.

a powerful civilization on the island of Crete. Maybe its rulers demanded that other people in the area pay taxes or send them something precious—perhaps even children. Child sacrifice wasn't unheard of in the Mediterranean, after all. It could be that the Cretans worshiped a bull-god (many religions had gods that looked like animals), and it might make sense for its priest to wear some kind of costume, making him look half human and half bull.

An Englishman named Sir Arthur Evans was fascinated with the stories about ancient Crete. In 1894, he bought some land near Knossos and started to dig. Almost immediately, he hit pay dirt: the remains of a huge palace, with a floor plan so elaborate that it looked like a maze. And painted on the walls were the symbols of power of the ruler: a double-headed axe.

Evans knew that a Greek word for "axe" was *labrus*. He was ecstatic! He was convinced he had found the labyrinth. He and his crew kept digging. They found room after room, with brightly-colored frescoes showing scenes of nature, beautiful women and handsome men, and geometric patterns. He found a large open area that he called "Ariadne's dancing floor." And in one room, he found two large and impressive chairs that reminded him of thrones. That was enough for him; he declared that this was Minos's palace and called the people who lived on Crete in the Bronze Age "Minoans."

BRONZE AGE

Bronze is an alloy, or mixture, of copper and tin. It is hard and holds a sharp edge better than any other metal that had been used before it was invented (or discovered). The Bronze Age (about 3000 BCE to 1000 BCE) refers to a period of time when this important metal helped shape trade, war, and art.

One of the frescoes shows a strange game or ritual. Huge bulls run at groups of athletes, both men and women, who run to meet the charging bull, grab it by the horns, and somersault onto its back before leaping off.

Could this be what Theseus and the other young Greek people were doing in Crete? Taking part in some kind of bull-leaping, either as a sport or as a sign of worship of a bull-god?

Evans thought so. He had walls built where he assumed they originally stood, and had artists fill in the blanks in damaged frescoes. Some of what he did was probably pretty accurate, but modern archaeologists know he made some mistakes. In any case, Evans's reconstructed palace at Knossos is spectacular and it is one of Greece's major tourist attractions today.

Some people aren't so sure that what Evans found has anything to do with a legendary king and a half-human monster who lived in a labyrinth. A beautiful large building certainly exists, however, and its basement is full of complicated passageways and grain-storage rooms. And the pictures do show people jumping over bulls.

The finds at Knossos raise even more questions than they answer. For instance, until the palace was excavated, most historians assumed that a king ruled over ancient Crete. But if there was a single leader, there ought to be some way of telling him apart from all the other people: a crown, a special robe, something. But all the people in the frescoes look about equal to each other. And then questions about the position of women in the society, the actual function of

In the Bronze Age, sporting events not only amused the onlookers but also tested the strength of warriors and often marked important ceremonies, such as funerals and victory celebrations. These boxers from the island of Thera don't look like serious athletes.

THE MYSTERY OF THE PHAISTOS DISK

In 1903, scholars were excited to find out about the discovery of a clay disk at Phaistos, the second-largest city of ancient Crete. This clay disk has symbols spiraling out from the center. Many efforts have been made to decipher it, without success. Oddly, the signs on the disk were made with stamps instead of being written. Some scholars find the object so strange that they have suggested that it might be a modern forgery. It could also be an import, and not Minoan at all. Another possibility is that the designs are not writing, but decoration.

the palace, and other questions started being raised. Archaeologists and historians are still working on finding out the answers.

Even when they get some answers, they might change their minds when new evidence is found and new archaeological techniques are invented. In fact, theories get changed all the time. One of them has to do with the island of Thera.

Sometime between 1700 and 1450 BCE, a minor Minoan outpost, the island of Thera (now called Santorini), blew up. Like the rest of the nearby islands, Thera was formed by a volcano. The earthquake produced by the eruption rocked the land for thousands of miles. Volcanic ash covered the sky, and perhaps blotted out the sun completely for days, and partially, for years. Tidal waves as high as 60 feet tall may have smashed into the coasts of nearby areas, including Crete.

Did the people of the area understand that a volcanic eruption is a natural event? Probably not. They probably thought that the gods were angry with them. This could have led to all sorts of religious, political, and social changes.

In 1939, an archaeologist named Spyridon Marinatos theorized that the eruption of Santorini caused Minoan civilization to fall, either because the economy couldn't survive the damage caused by the ash and the lack of sun, or because the people's confidence in their leaders was shaken.

Some archaeologists and historians did not accept that theory because the Minoan civilization continued for 150 years after the eruption. More recently, however, geologists have learned that the explosion was even bigger than had previously been thought. It was so enormous that it might have disrupted trade through the entire Mediterranean region. A geologist named William Ryan suggested in 2003 that a ripple effect caused by the effect of the ash on different parts of the Mediterranean world could eventually have led to the fall of the Minoan civilization.

Whether it was the fault of the volcano, some other as yet unknown factor, or a combination the power of the Minoans declined, until by the 15th century BCE, a new force was ready to take control of the Mediterranean. These people were the mighty Mycenaeans.

CHAPTER 4

A GREAT CIVILIZATION IS BORN

MIGHTY MYCENAEANS

It's 3,000 years in the future. Archaeologists are excavating the remains of an advanced civilization. They uncover a great city with houses, roads, works of art, mysterious machines, and magnificent monuments. They also find flat pieces of a plant-based material, usually white, covered with black squiggles. The scientists think that there used to be many more of these, but that most of them were destroyed in the calamity that brought down the civilization.

It occurs to someone that the squiggles must have held meaning for the people, now vanished, who once lived in this great city. A scholar works for years deciphering them, and finally, she cracks the code! In her hand she holds the first precious words translated from that long-dead language. They are:

Lettuce
Bread
Crackers
Spaghetti sauce

Can you imagine the archaeologist's disappointment? After all her work, it turns out that what she has been struggling to understand was nothing but a shopping list.

This is what happened to an Englishman named Michael Ventris in 1953. Even as a child, Ventris was so interested in ancient

The Lion Gate marked the entrance to Mycenae. The powerful lions symbolized the strength of the city's rulers.

hieros + glyphein =
"sacred" + "carving"
Ancient Egyptians carved
hieroglyphs on monuments.

languages that at the age of eight he bought himself a book about Egyptian **hieroglyphs**. When he was 14, he went to hear Sir Arthur Evans, the excavator of the huge palace at the city of Knossos on the island of Crete, give a lecture about some mysterious clay tablets. Evans and his team had found dozens of these small objects in palaces on Crete and the Greek mainland. Symbols were cut into or painted on them in straight lines. Evans called the writing "Linear B."

After the lecture, Ventris went up to Sir Arthur and said, "Did you say they've never been deciphered, Sir?" Sir Arthur told him that this was so. Ventris was hooked.

As an adult, Ventris became an architect. But in his spare time, he kept up his interest in the tablets. When photographs and drawings of them became available, he wrote letters to other people all over the world who were also interested in deciphering Linear B.

Ventris wrote out copies of his research notes and sent them to these other people, who sent comments back to him. They gave him some helpful ideas, but it was slow going.

"Archaic" comes from
archaios, which means
"extremely old." It especially
refers to an early period
of a culture.

Finally, Ventris decided to see if the language was a kind of **archaic** Greek. He didn't have much hope, though. Almost everybody thought that Greek civilization had not yet reached the island of Crete where most of the Linear B writing had been found. He said in a note to the people who were helping him out, "I suspect that this line of decipherment would sooner or later come to an impasse or dissipate itself in absurdities."

To Ventris's surprise, when he substituted Greek letters for the Linear B symbols, he started finding words that sounded like Greek. At last, he could read the deathless words and important thoughts of these long-vanished people. And what did he first read?

A list of seventy oxen.

Ventris then realized that he wasn't going to read some great tale or interesting history on the clay tablets. Still, he was excited—he had the key. He wrote to a friend, "I have, I think, great news for you. You must judge for yourself, but I think I've deciphered Linear B." He went on to say that the language was Greek.

Sir Arthur Evans found this clay tablet in 1900 at the palace of Knossos and called the script Linear B. At that time, nobody could read it, but in 1953, an English architect, Michael Ventris, deciphered it and found that Linear B was an early version of Greek.

Many of the tablets contained lists. One said:

For chariots: 18 men, for wheels: 18 men
For flint points: 13 men, for halters: 5 men
For shafts [of spears]: 36 men

❝ Linear B Tablet from the Palace of Knossos, about 1200 BCE

Even from this short list, historians can figure out some information. The people who wrote Linear B knew how to make chariots and must have been preparing for hunting or battle. Other tablets and painted pots have yielded more facts.

Once Ventris and other scholars were able to translate the tablets, they found out more about the Minoans, as recorded in Linear B tablets (written by their Mycenaean conquerors). For one thing, just the fact that the Minoans kept lists shows that they had an organized society. They thought it was important to keep track of things like how many pieces of equipment were made by particular artisans, who owned them, and where they were stored.

Other clues found in the excavations on Crete told the archaeologists that at some time in the 15th century BCE, the Mycenaeans, who were based in mainland Greece, conquered Crete. They moved a force into Knossos and ruled the island from there. It must have been an unhappy time for the Minoans. They had controlled the Mediterranean, and now they were being controlled by the Mycenaeans, who used to pay them tribute, or tax.

INVENTING A WRITTEN LANGUAGE

Michael Ventris wasn't the only person trying to decipher Linear B. But he was the first one to think that it might be a syllabary, and this was his big breakthrough in cracking the code.

A syllabary is a system of writing in which each symbol stands for a consonant-vowel cluster. The language spoken by the members of the Cherokee Nation is a very old one, but its written form goes back only to 1821. That was the year in which the Cherokee Sequoia (also known as George Guess) made a syllabary for his language. Other languages, such as the ancient Egyptian hieroglyphs, are written with a syllabary instead of an alphabet.

The Mycenaeans didn't just rule over the conquered Cretans, though. They learned from them. And one important thing they learned was writing.

The Mycenaeans, who didn't have a written language of their own, used the symbols of the syllabary of the Cretan script, now called Linear A, to write their own language. This is what we call Linear B, the script that Michael Ventris translated in 1953.

Writing must have been so exciting, and must have given the newly literate people so much power that it is no wonder the Mycenaeans suddenly produced many clay tablets. (They probably wrote on parchment and wax, too, but these materials are more fragile and have all disappeared.) By piecing together evidence from different tablets, the archaeologists have figured out some details about the Mycenaean civilization. They found out, for example, that a *wanax*, or a leader, ruled over lower officials. People had to pay taxes. Wool and flax were important, and women did the spinning and the weaving. Slaves, bronze-workers, and furniture makers are listed, although most people were farmers.

Although the first tablets excavated were found on Crete, most Mycenaean settlements were in mainland Greece. Archaeologists excavated large palaces at the center of each citadel on the Greek mainland. They unearthed enormous walls that were specially designed to protect the cities. They found that the Mycenaeans had dug big water tanks so that in case a city was attacked, the people could lock themselves inside and still have enough water to live on.

Gold cups like this one from Sparta illustrate the wealth of aristocrats from the Peloponnesus in the Bronze Age and show that the poet Homer knew some details about this era: he describes a cup much like this one.

Beehive tombs are a style of Mycenaean tomb. They were covered with dirt, which created a mound with most of the tomb underground, and were connected to the surface by a long tunnel that leads to a door. Inside the tomb, the main circular room was probably used for rituals, and the body was interred in a smaller chamber to the side.

Scholars discovered that the Mycenaeans grew wealthier and more powerful as they traded all over their known world. Their pottery has been found in the western Mediterranean, Egypt, Anatolia (present-day Turkey), Syria, and Cyprus.

Then around 1100 BCE, most of the Mycenaean cities were destroyed or abandoned. What could have happened? Some scientists think there was an epidemic, an uprising of the peasants against the *wanax,* or an invasion by some foreign powers. Perhaps it was a combination of these.

Michael Ventris's life also had a sudden and unexpected end. In 1956, when he was only 34 years old and before he had finished translating the Linear B tablets, he was killed in a car accident. He never saw his book, *Documents in Mycenaean Greek,* which was published just a few weeks after his death.

WHAT'S A *WANAX*?

To the writers of Linear B, a *wanax* was a leader. By the time the poet Homer was writing about their civilization, the word had lost its "w" and its meaning had changed slightly to "overlord" or "boss." Homer called Zeus *anax andron te theon te* ("ruler of men and of gods"), and Agamemnon, the mythical king of Mycenae, *anax andron* ("ruler of men").

ALWAYS LOOK A GIFT HORSE IN THE BELLY
THE TROJAN WAR

The expression "Never look a gift horse in the mouth" means that if someone gives you a present, you should just take it and not look too closely to see if there's anything wrong with it.

But sometimes it pays to check out a gift. If you were at war for years and years, and thousands of enemy soldiers kept trying to break into your city, wouldn't you be suspicious if all but one of them suddenly disappeared? And if they left a huge wooden horse outside your city walls, and their only remaining soldier said it was a present, you might think that there was more to this weird gift than a sudden attack of generosity.

This was the situation that the people of Troy (also called Ilion) found themselves in. According to the myths, it all started when Paris, a Trojan prince, was asked to give a gold apple to the most beautiful goddess. Aphrodite said that if he chose her, she would give him the most beautiful woman in

The creator of this pot showed the Trojan horse with wheels, making it easy for it to enter the city.

the world. (They thought that a goddess could just give people away.)

Paris thought that Aphrodite's offer was the best, so he chose her. His reward was the celebrated beauty, Helen.

One problem was that Helen was already married to a Mycenaean king, Menelaus of Sparta. But Paris didn't care—he just went to Sparta, picked up Helen, and went back to Troy.

Menelaus asked his powerful brother Agamemnon and other Greek leaders to help him get his wife back. They set sail for Troy and tried to break through the high city walls. Many famous warriors and courageous but unnamed soldiers, as well as civilians, died on both sides. According to the Greek epic the *Iliad,* the Trojans and Greeks fought for ten years.

Also according to the *Iliad,* Paris's brother Hector felt especially pessimistic about the Trojans' prospects for winning the war. During a break from the fighting, he says to his beloved wife,

> For I know this thing well in my heart, and my mind
>   knows it:
> There will come a day when sacred Ilion shall perish.

He imagined his parents and his brothers dying at the hands of their enemies. But what upset him the most was the thought of his wife becoming the slave of a Greek soldier:

> And some day seeing you shedding tears a man will
>   say of you:
> "This is the wife of Hector, who was ever the bravest
>   fighter
> Of the Trojans, breaker of horses, in the days when
>   they fought about Ilion." . . .
> But may I be dead and the piled earth hide me under
>   before I
> Hear you crying and know by this that they drag you
>   captive.

The war dragged on. It looked as though neither side would ever win. But then the wily Greek hero Odysseus

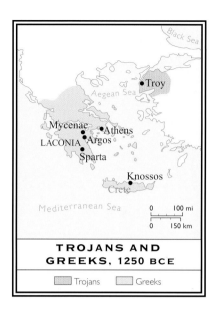

TROJANS AND GREEKS, 1250 BCE

Trojans   Greeks

66 Homer, *Iliad,* about 750 BCE

"Trojan horse" now means something that looks harmless, but can cause damage. One computer virus was called the Trojan Horse Virus.

thought of building a huge horse and hiding some soldiers in it. He hoped that the Trojans would like the horse so much that they would drag it inside the city walls.

The Trojans fell for it, and they opened their gates. They pulled the horse inside. Later that night, after the people of Troy had all gone to bed, one of the Greek soldiers opened a secret door in the belly of the **Trojan horse**. Soldiers poured out into the dark city.

Hector's gloomy prediction came true. The Greeks slaughtered most of the sleeping Trojans, and imprisoned others for future use as slaves. Then they burned down the city, killing everyone who couldn't get away in time. The Greeks went home in triumph.

There's a lot more to the story of the Trojan War than the episode of the horse and the fall of Troy. In fact, the ancient Greeks thought that the two books that tell the story of Troy and Odysseus, Homer's *Iliad* and *Odyssey*, contained just about everything an educated person needed to know. You want to build a boat? Read descriptions of great ships in them. You need to study geography? Read the list of Greek ships and where they came from in the *Iliad*. Even manners were covered. How should a naked man behave when he accidentally stumbles upon a princess and her friends playing ball? (To see how Odysseus handled this embarrassing situation, see the *Odyssey*, Book VI.)

For many centuries, people wondered if the story of the Trojan War was a made-up legend, or if it

A prophet named Laocoön warned the Trojans not to take the horse inside the walls. But before he could get anyone to listen, some snakes swam out of the sea and strangled him along with at least one of his sons. The sculptor of this huge statue shows another son escaping. He is on the right, slipping the snake's coils off his leg.

had some basis in fact. By modern times, most people thought it was just an exciting story. One of the few people who was convinced that it was based on a real war was a man named Heinrich Schliemann.

When he was seven years old (in 1829), Schliemann was fascinated by a book that had a picture of Troy burning down. He made up his mind to find what remained of the city.

He read and reread the *Iliad* and the *Odyssey* until he figured out where he thought he could find Troy. He decided that it must lie under a mound of dirt near a town called Hissarlik in present-day Turkey.

Most people laughed at him. But they stopped laughing when Schliemann, digging at Hissarlik, struck a rich treasure of gold jewelry. It was in a layer of the mound that looked as though it had been where a great city had once stood—a city that had been destroyed by fire. He was convinced it was the Troy of the *Iliad*. Schliemann smuggled the jewelry out of Turkey. The Turks were furious, and they refused to allow him to return to the site at Hissarlik.

While Schliemann was waiting for the Turks to change their minds, he went to Greece, to where he thought Mycenae must be, to look for the tombs of Agamemnon and his wife Clytemnestra (Helen's sister). Once again, luck was on his side. Almost immediately, he found a group of graves. The gold and other treasures that he found in the graves proved that very powerful people were buried there. Schliemann was thrilled. He was sure they were the graves of ancient kings and queens—maybe even the very ones he was looking for.

After a while, the Turkish government allowed Schliemann to return to Hissarlik and continue his excavation. He kept digging there until he died, sure that he had found Troy.

But not everyone was convinced. From the start, some people said that Schliemann was wrong. They said that the part of Hissarlik where he had found the treasure was from 1,000 years before the war that Homer wrote about, and that the tombs that he hoped were of Agamemnon and Clytemnestra were also from the wrong time. Most modern archaeologists agree with them, and add that it looks like

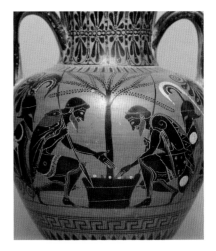

The great Greek warriors Achilles and Ajax are letting the Trojans think that they are so relaxed that they are going to play a board game. They are showing off, though. They're not relaxed enough to take off their armor before picking up the dice!

EVERYBODY'S GOT A SORE SPOT

The greatest Greek warrior in the Trojan War was Achilles. He was the son of a mortal man and the goddess Thetis. His mother dipped him in the River Styx to make sure that he would be immortal, like her. But she held him by the heel and the heel never got wet, making this his vulnerable spot. Guess where an arrow hit him during the Trojan War? The expression "Achilles' heel" means a weakness that can cause harm.

Was Helen Innocent?

The historian Herodotus didn't believe that Helen was the cause of the Trojan War. When Herodotus was in Egypt, he heard that when Paris was sailing to Troy with Helen, he was shipwrecked on the Egyptian coast. When the Egyptian priests heard that Paris had kidnapped the wife of a man who had been his host, they were outraged. One of them told him he had to depart right away, leaving behind everything he had stolen from Sparta, including Helen.

Herodotus seemed to think that this story made sense, writing in the *Histories*:

"*I* myself am in agreement with this version of the story, especially when you bear in mind that if Helen had been in Troy, she would certainly have been surrendered to the Greeks whether Paris liked it or not, for neither Priam nor any member of his household was crazy enough to risk being ruined along with their children and their city just so Paris could have Helen for his wife.*"

Schliemann made up some of the entries in his diary, where he wrote about what he had found each day. Some even say that the "mask of Agamemnon" is a modern forgery, or that some parts like the beard were added later. Most archaeologists agree that Schliemann was careless and destroyed many beautiful and interesting artifacts and important buildings in his eager search for Troy.

What's the truth? Was there ever a Trojan War? If so, when and where did it happen? And why? If the fighting wasn't over Helen, what was the cause of the war?

Often, wars are fought for economic reasons. Many scholars think that the Trojan War happened around 1200 BCE, when Greece was probably being invaded by strangers from the north. The Greeks might have been looking for new places to trade to take the place of the countries they could no longer get to during the invasions. Maybe they were seeking places to send colonists.

It's possible that we'll never know. But sometimes things turn up when you least expect them. Archaeologists thought for years that the Trojan jewelry that Schliemann found was lost during World War II. Some said it was melted down to make new jewelry. But in 1994, a team of researchers found it in a museum in Moscow.

Who knows? Maybe someday an archaeologist working at Hissarlik or some other spot will dig up a giant horseshoe, or a helmet saying "I belong to Hector." Maybe you will be that archaeologist.

Nobody knows the name of the king in whose grave this solid-gold mask was found. Heinrich Schliemann thought he knew who it was, however. When he first saw it, he exclaimed, "I have gazed on the face of Agamemnon!"

CHAPTER 6

SING, MUSE
EARLY POETS

The Greeks believed that the nine Muses, daughters of Apollo, helped them to write poetry. This statue base shows three of the Muses.

Y ou have to memorize a story, with lots of characters and suspense and a complicated plot. The story is so long that if you start to tell it right now, you will finish tomorrow at around this same time. While you are telling it, you might close your eyes for long periods to help the details come to mind. In fact, if you are blind, you might find you have an advantage over sighted people: not only are you less distracted by the world around you, but you've always had to rely on your memory. So you already know some tricks about how to remember things.

If you sing something, and especially if the song has a strong rhythm, it's easier to memorize. Three-year-olds can sing the ABC song even before they know what letters are for.

Repetition also helps. Many people can sing "Take Me Out to the Ball Game," but the part that they know is just the chorus—hardly anyone knows the rest of the words because the chorus is the part repeated most often.

"Poet" comes from *poetes*, which means "maker."

In ancient Greece, few people could read (even fewer could write). So it's only natural that an ancient Greek would think that a great **poet**, one capable of inventing and then reciting an exciting, beautiful poem 16,000 lines long, might well be blind. To make it easier to remember, the poem would probably be sung, or at least chanted to a strong rhythm, and it would help if it had lots of repetition. Melody was so tied with poetry that the Greek word *mousike*, from which we get the English word music, means both "music" *and* "poetry."

So the Greeks thought that Homer, the poet they said composed the *Iliad* and the *Odyssey*, was blind. It's possible that he was, but there's no way of knowing that for sure, or even whether both poems were written by the same person and what his name really was.

If a blind poet named Homer really did compose the *Odyssey*, he put what appears to be a self-portrait in his story. In the description of a dinner-party, a blind poet is led in to take a seat and entertain the guests:

66 Homer, *Odyssey*, about 725 BCE

> The herald came near, bringing with him the
>   excellent singer
> Whom the Muse had loved greatly. . . .
> She had deprived him of his sight, but she gave him
>   the sweet singing art. . . .
> The herald hung the clear lyre on a peg placed over
> His head, and showed him how to reach up with his
>   hands and take it down.

In any case, the author (or authors) of the *Iliad* and the *Odyssey* was not the first Greek poet. He was, however, the first whose poetry got written down. Most people think that the *Iliad* (the earlier of the two books) was written in

THE ALPHABET

The first two letters in the Greek alphabet are *alpha* and *beta*—that's why we call the group of letters used in a language an "alphabet." Writing came to Greece in the ninth century BCE. The Greek alphabet is similar to the Roman alphabet, which is used in most of Europe and the Americas.

GREEK		ROMAN	
UPPERCASE	LOWERCASE	UPPERCASE	LOWERCASE
A	α	A	a
B	β	B	b
Δ	δ	D	d

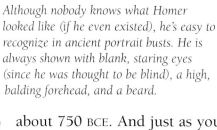

Although nobody knows what Homer looked like (if he even existed), he's easy to recognize in ancient portrait busts. He is always shown with blank, staring eyes (since he was thought to be blind), a high, balding forehead, and a beard.

about 750 BCE. And just as you would suspect, both poems have a strong rhythm and repetition.

Poetry must have seemed like magic. Not only the audience, but sometimes even the poet himself thought that it was impossible to compose something so beautiful and to remember it so well without divine help. The Greeks thought that poets were aided by the nine Muses, daughters of Apollo (god of the arts) and a nymph named Mnemosyne. An early poet named Hesiod gave the Muses credit for his great verses in his book *The Theogony*:

One day the Muses taught me glorious song. . . .
They plucked and gave to me a laurel rod,
A sturdy shoot, a truly wondrous thing,
And into me they breathed a voice divine
To celebrate the future and the past.
My orders were to celebrate the gods who live
Eternally, but most of all to sing
Of them themselves, the Muses, first and last.

But why did the ancient Greeks admire poets so much? Most ancient Greeks had very little free time, since they had a lot of work to do. But they didn't work *every* minute. When they were through with their work for the day, many of them probably played a game or made music. They loved sports, and music was popular.

> ## YOU SPELL THAT WITH AN "M," AS IN MNEMOSYNE
>
> *Mnemosyne* (the first "m" is silent) was the name of the Muses' mother and is the Greek word for memory. A mnemonic device is a trick to help you remember something. To help you with the names of the nine Muses use the mnemonic device "MUP, ETC., ETC." It gives you a clue to Melpomene, Urania, Polyhymnia, Erato, Terpsichore, Clio, Euterpe, Thalia, and Calliope.

❝ Hesiod, *The Theogony*, about 700 BCE

Much of Sappho's poetry exists today only on scraps like this second-century CE papyrus. Since many Greeks lived in Egypt, starting especially in the late fourth century BCE, much of what we know of Greek literature comes from there. Sometimes the poems were written on linen that was later used as mummy-wrappings, and when archaeologists unwind the cloth, they find works of literature on it.

Storytelling was also a great way to pass the time. People who could memorize long tales and tell them well were probably as well treated as the poet mentioned in the *Odyssey*. Hearing these stories was an important way that Greeks learned about their history (or an entertaining version of it). They could be proud of the great Greek heroes, like Achilles. They could feel united against enemies, remembering that they all shared a great Greek heritage.

Not all poems were about warriors and their brave deeds. One poet questioned whether honor was really that important. Losing a shield, for example, was not only expensive but a disgrace, because when soldiers surrendered to an enemy, they handed over their armor, including their shields. But a poet named Archilochus had a different point of view:

66 Archilochus, untitled poem, about 650 BCE

> Well, some barbarian's glad to have the shield
> I had to leave behind—a nice one, too—
> Thrown underneath a bush. But I'm alive!
> I got away—the hell with that old shield!
> I'll get another some day just as good.

A poem could be a curse, as in this one by Sappho, the Greeks' favorite female poet:

> You will die and be still, never shall be memory left
>   of you
> After this, nor regret when you are gone. You have
>   not touched the flowers
> Of the Muses, and thus, shadowy still in the domain
>   of Death,
> You must drift with a ghost's fluttering wings, one of
>   the darkened dead.

❝ Sappho, untitled poem, about 600 BCE

Many poets wrote about love and loneliness. This one is also probably by Sappho:

> The moon has gone, the stars have set, the night is
>   halfway done,
> And here I lie as time goes by—alone, alone, alone.

❝ Sappho, untitled poem, about 600 BCE

epi + *taphos* =
"upon" + "a tomb"
An epitaph is a tomb inscription or short statement commemorating a dead person.

Epitaphs were usually in verse form, too. The poet Simonides wrote a short but moving tribute to the Spartans who died fighting the Persians:

> Go tell the Spartans, stranger passing by,
> That here, obeying their commands, we lie.

❝ Simonides, Epitaph for Spartan soldiers, early fifth century BCE

It might seem that nowadays, poetry isn't as important as it was for the Greeks. But we probably hear more poems than the Greeks ever did. We call them "songs" because they're set to music, but so was most Greek poetry. Our songs serve the same purposes that Greek poetry did. Our national anthems make us feel united. We sing special songs on special days: "Happy Birthday to You," "Auld Lang Syne," and many others. Love songs tell people we care about them. Marching songs help encourage soldiers to be brave. Greek poetry was used in the same ways.

CHAPTER 7

GREECE SPREADS ITS WINGS
COLONIES AND CITY-STATES

❝ An inscription of a Greek law from Cyrene, late seventh century BCE

If anyone is unwilling to sail when sent by the city, let him be subject to the death penalty and let his property be confiscated. Whoever receives or protects such a person—whether a father his son or a brother his brother—shall suffer the same punishment as the person who refused to sail.

It seems harsh to put someone to death for refusing to sail to a new colony. What's going on here?

Things were changing in the Greek world. When the glorious days of the Minoan and Mycenaean civilizations ended, many ways of life were altered in the lands around the Aegean Sea. We call that time (1200–750 BCE) the "Dark Age," partly because we know so little about it that it seems shadowy to us, and partly because what we do know appears very gloomy. In the Dark Age, most people in Greece were very poor. The population dropped, leaving some areas deserted. No large constructions like the palaces on Crete and in Mycenae were built, and very little art was produced. There isn't any Greek literature from that time period—in fact, it appears that for hundreds of years the entire culture forgot how to read and write. After the collapse of the palaces, there were no records to keep and nobody to pay the scribes who kept them.

The rulers of most early Greek cultures claimed they were descended from the gods, or from a particular god. Toward the end of the Dark Age this changed, and people

Cups like this enable historians to understand what Greek ships looked like. Founding colonies was so important for the Greeks that the state could execute a person who refused to sail off to a new place in a colonization venture.

were no longer governed by one powerful ruler. Instead, small groups of landowning men took over. They called their form of government an **aristocracy** because they thought they were better than everyone else. The rest of the people, who felt unfairly excluded from ruling, called it an **oligarchy**.

aristos + cratia = "best" + "rule" Government by the people best suited to rule.

oligos + archein = "few" + "to rule" Government by a few people.

The Dark Age gave way to what we call the Archaic period. Greece was changing once more and so were Greek ways of looking at the world. The Archaic period wasn't a dark age at all. People made beautiful statues and wrote poetry. They asked questions about society.

Many of these questions concerned the best form of government. By the time the Archaic age was over, around 550 BCE, the Greeks had organized themselves into hundreds of little countries (probably more than 1,000), each of which was called a *polis*.

There's no exact equivalent for the word *polis* in English, so we have to call it a city-state—a small area governed by a central town or city. A *polis* usually comprised fewer than 10,000 people (Athens and Corinth were huge by Greek standards, with about 100,000 inhabitants, as far as historians can tell).

Each *polis* had to be fairly self-sufficient, governing itself, providing most of its own food and other supplies and protecting itself from enemies. The Greek terrain made this necessary. Even today, it's hard to get from one part of Greece to another. On a map a distance may not seem too great, but with so many mountains to go around, you can drive and drive without getting very far at all. The same journey on foot or on a donkey would take an adventurous person or a person in desperate need of something. One *polis* would have problems trying to control settlements separated by such difficult roads. So each *polis* had to rely on itself.

The *polis* was politically independent. It had everything that defines a nation today: a government, laws, customs. Every *polis* had a sort of capital—a central town or village— and included land around it. Most *poleis* (the plural of *polis*) had an acropolis—a high fortified part of the city—and an agora—an open-air gathering-place. Most of all, a *polis* was

The "Antikythera Mechanism" (found in 1901 in the sea off the island of Antikythera) was probably made around 65 BCE. The clock-like device calculated the motions of stars and planets and was used to navigate ships. It has been called an ancient computer.

inhabited by people who thought about the best form of government and tried to put it into practice. One aspect they questioned was the system of oligarchy.

Historians are very eager to know how this thinking developed. Why did people stop just accepting government by oligarchs?

The answer lies in more than one area. Political and economic life are interconnected. During the years of relative peace under the oligarchs, the population grew. Greece's rocky islands and mountains leave little ground that can be farmed, especially when there are more people to be fed. It became impossible for one *polis* to support itself entirely. Aside from food, people had to think of new ways to acquire goods that their *polis* couldn't supply. So some people took up trading. At the same time, better navigational instruments were invented that helped sailors to travel farther away from home.

But what does this have to do with getting rid of the oligarchs?

For one thing, it meant that some Greeks decided to leave their native states and go to other parts of the world and set up colonies. Between 750 and 550 BCE, thousands of people spread out in all directions from mainland Greece.

The Acropolis still dominates modern Athens. The word acropolis means "high city" and many ancient Greek city-states were built around it, so the residents could seek refuge there in times of invasion.

Travel gave the Greek colonists different perspectives on life and opened their minds to new ideas.

When they arrived in their new homes, the colonists had to come up with new ways of governing themselves. Many colonists thought an oligarchy wasn't the best way to run their new settlements. They preferred to have the best rulers, not ones descended from earlier leaders. And when visitors to the colonies returned home, they talked about what they had seen in the new settlements. The idea of a different type of government intrigued the people in the home states. More and more *poleis* sprang up, both in the colonies and back in the homeland.

The Greeks also picked up other ideas. For example, in Lydia, a country on the west coast of what is now Turkey, the government had begun issuing coins. Greek *poleis* were so impressed with this great idea that they started doing the same thing. It was much easier to buy and sell things with a piece of metal stamped with the symbol of a strong *polis* that you could trust—and much more convenient to purchase cargo with a sack of coins than to go home and fetch six cows to exchange.

Colonies spread further as the need for land and trade increased, just as they would centuries later when Europeans

THE *POLIS* IN ENGLISH

Polis gives us many English words: politics, political, polity, and others. Since the Greeks tended to think of people who lived in the country as less refined or less sophisticated than city-dwellers, you might think that "polite" comes from *polis*. However, the Latin word *politus* ("polished") is its real ancestor. If a *polis* of 10,000 people seems too small to have been called a separate country, just think of the smallest country in the modern world: Vatican City. In 2001, its population was only 890 people!

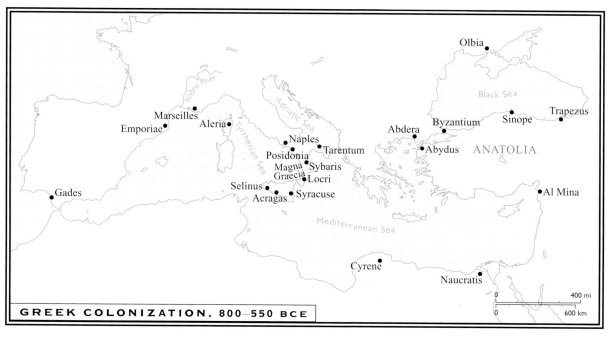

GREEK COLONIZATION, 800–550 BCE

founded colonies in the Americas. Many Greeks went off to establish trading posts in Syria and Egypt.

All sorts of resources were found in the colonies, such as timber, crops, and metal. In the *Odyssey*, the goddess Athena disguised herself as a metal trader. The poet Homer said that she told people who were curious about why she was sailing around, "I have come here with my ship and crew . . . with a cargo of iron, and I shall bring back copper." Everyone in the story believed her, which shows that this kind of trade was common.

Homer, *Odyssey*, about 725 BCE

When the colonists established their new homes, it must have been exhilarating. They finally had enough land to make a living and they were making their own new *poleis*. The Greeks thought that many of their cities had been founded by gods or mythical heroes, and here they were, just normal people, doing the same thing.

These *poleis* spread all around the Mediterranean, leading to a kind of network of Greek city-states. Although they were so far apart from each other—or maybe *because* they were so far apart—the colonists remained proudly Greek. They continued to speak their own language. They worshiped the

Greek gods. They built temples that looked like the ones at home—in fact, some of the most beautiful Greek temples are in Sicily. They brought their favorite crops to the new lands. Nowadays, for example, Italy is the world's largest producer of wine. But no grapes grew in Italy until the Greek colonists planted them there.

In fact, Italy was so heavily colonized that it became almost another Greece. It even became known as "Magna Graecia"—greater Greece.

Once they arrived in their new home, the colonists had a lot to do. In the *Odyssey* Homer describes the task of the leader of a new colony:

> He led a crowd of folk to Scheria. . . .
> Around the city he had placed a wall.
> He had made houses; also for the gods
> He saw to it that there were temples, and the land
> He carefully divided up.

❝ Homer, *Odyssey*, about 725 BCE

The Greeks not only had recovered from the Dark Age, but also had developed the *polis*, a political unit that would change and grow into a form that would change much of the world. The Greek world had expanded to create a vibrant, far-flung, and prosperous civilization.

That prosperity, however, came with a price. Just because Greeks had been thinking about and experimenting with government didn't mean that they had solved all the problems of living in communities. In earlier times, prosperity had come only from land. Now there was another route to wealth: trade. Conflict often erupted between those who had made their money in agriculture and the successful merchants. And not everybody was prosperous. In some places, those who were still poor were unhappier than ever, seeing the success of others.

It was impossible to be certain what was going to happen next, but the people who guessed there would be revolutions and civil wars were on the right track.

Some temples in Greek colonies are in better shape than those in Greece itself, partly because they are made of less-valuable material than the highly prized marble, which would have been plundered to be used in another building. That the temple of Segesta in Sicily was built using the honey-colored local stone may have spared it from being plundered.

CHAPTER 8

WHO'S IN CHARGE HERE?
THE RISE OF ATHENS

Solon, *Elegies*, early sixth
century BCE

Each man exerts himself differently:
One, tempest-tossed, travels the fishy sea
Hoping to bring some profit home,
Risking exhaustion, even death.
Another plows the wooded land year in, year out,
Working for hire, caring for the curved plows.
One . . . earns his living with his hands,
Another becomes wonderfully wise;
Another has become a prophet thanks to Lord Apollo.

When the Athenian poet and politician Solon wrote these words, his hometown was in sorry shape. People became leaders by being born into the ruling class, not by being best able to govern. With their political power and their wealth, the rich leaders could easily drive the poorer farmers out of business. Bankrupt farmers sometimes had to sell themselves into slavery in order for their families to survive.

The people of the middle classes—craftsmen, traders, and prosperous farmers—weren't quite as badly off as the bankrupt farmers, but they were kept out of the government and resented their exclusion.

In some Greek *poleis*, problems like these had led to revolutions and tyrannies. The Athenians were worried that the same might happen in their *polis*, so they took an unusual step: in about 600 BCE they decided to entrust one wise, honest man with the task of straightening things out. This man would be allowed to do whatever he thought was necessary, without having to get approval from anyone else. They settled on

Solon (who later became known as one of the "Seven Wise Men of Greece") as the best man for the job.

Solon's immediate concern was the economy. One of his first accomplishments was to cancel the land debts that had forced people into slavery. This didn't make Solon many friends in the upper classes, but he had more important matters to deal with than the anger of a few rich landowners.

Next, Solon passed a law freeing all the Athenians who had become enslaved. He later wrote of this accomplishment with obvious pride:

The scene on this krater, *a jar or a vase, shows a pottery workshop, where skilled artisans made pots, dishes, and vases. Well-made pottery was so highly prized that people requested wares made by a specific craftsman and painted by a certain painter.*

> I brought back to their native city, god-built Athens,
> Those who had been sold, . . . and as for those
> Who suffered shameful slavery here at home
> And trembled daily at their masters' whims,
> I made them free too.

66 Solon, *Elegies*, early sixth century BCE

Another of his important acts was to encourage trading. This was the start of Athens's importance as a trading center.

Solon also developed a system based on dividing society into four classes. How much income a man made determined which class he and his family were in. Men from the two highest classes could hold the most important government positions. Men from the third class could hold lower offices.

Up until then, class was determined by birth: if your father was upper class, so were you, no matter how much (or how little) money you earned. And what was truly revolutionary was Solon's declaration that free men from *all* social classes could vote and serve on juries. (It didn't occur to anyone that women should be allowed to vote. That came much

Athena is the goddess of war and patron deity of Athens. As goddess of war, she wears a helmet.

later—thousands of years later, in most countries.) The jury system meant that the community was more involved in legal decisions than in the old system, where a single judge could decide guilt or innocence and punishment.

demos + cratia =
"people" + "rule"
"Democracy" means "rule by the people."

Modern definitions of the word **democracy** tell us that in this system, people of different social classes and income levels all have the same rights. So it might seem that Solon's reforms didn't really lead to democracy. But before Solon, when all that mattered was what family you came from, there was no chance for a poor man to move up in the world. Solon's system, which was based on income instead of birth, gave people a reason to work harder: to get a bigger role in politics.

Not everyone was thrilled with Solon's reforms. Many aristocrats were angry that somebody from a lower social class could catch up to them politically. And throughout history, people from all sections of society sometimes have difficulty with change, even if the change looks as if it will make their lives better.

So other forms of government were tested in Athens and elsewhere. During the transition between the rule of the oligarchs and the growth of the *poleis*, many times it wasn't clear who was running things. In some cases, a powerful man seized power from the oligarchs, often with the support of the middle and lower classes. He was known as a *tyrannos*, or "tyrant." Today, the word "tyrant" means a ruler who governs in an oppressive, unjust, or cruel way. But to the Greeks, a *tyrannos* was originally just a ruler with absolute power—one who came into power by seizing it, not by being born into it or elected.

The tyrant didn't have to obey any rules. The Greeks didn't think that there was necessarily anything bad about this. Naturally, some tyrants abused their power. This wasn't always the case, however, and some tyrants were apparently good rulers. Some Greeks were relieved to have the oligarchs out of the way and gladly supported a tyrant who got into power because of his personality and strengths, not by just happening to be born into the right family. They also knew that a tyrant had to keep the people happy, or they would stop supporting him and either establish a different form of government or help another tyrant take his place.

One of the most successful tyrants was a clever Athenian named Peisistratus. He first got into power by wounding himself and his mules and then asking for bodyguards to protect him from his (imaginary) enemies. He used these bodyguards to help him seize power. He ruled Athens for about five years and then was kicked out. This was always a risk for tyrants—they made enemies easily. But he came up with a plan to get back into power: he got a tall, beautiful woman to dress in armor, and she drove a chariot into Athens. The historian Herodotus wrote in his *Histories*:

> As they approached the city, the criers . . . shouted, "Athenians! Give a warm welcome to Peisistratus! Athena has honored him above all other men and is herself bringing him back to her own acropolis!" . . . [T]he city dwellers, in the belief that this woman was the goddess herself, worshiped a human being and welcomed Peisistratus.

66 Herodotus, *Histories*, mid-fifth century BCE

Herodotus said that he could hardly believe that people as smart as the Athenians fell for such a ridiculous trick.

THE SWORD
OF DAMOCLES

One powerful tyrant was Dionysius of Syracuse in Sicily, who was so free from the customary rules of Greek society that one day he married two women in a single ceremony. When his friend Damocles expressed jealousy of a tyrant's freedom, Dionysius set before him a beautiful table filled with delicious food. At first Damocles was delighted, but when he looked up, he was horrified to see a sharp sword dangling over his neck attached only to a thread. This way Dionysius, who had many enemies, showed that having great power also placed a man in great danger.

As the symbol of Athena, the owl was a wise choice for an image on this Athenian coin of the late sixth or early fifth century BCE.

As tyrant, Peisistratus was most interested in building up the Athenian economy. He loaned money and even gave away land to people who needed it. He encouraged the export of pottery, one of the greatest Athenian crafts. Athenian pottery from the age of Peisistratus has been found as far away as Spain and Syria. This increased trade helped Athens become even more powerful.

Peisistratus or one of his sons was the first ruler to mint the silver coins with the face of Athena on one side and an owl on the other that became the most trusted money in the Greek world. People knew that this coin was pure silver and worth as much money as it was supposed to represent, so many preferred Athenian coins to any other.

Peisistratus also supported the arts. He paid for temples to be built and for plays to be performed. During his reign, vase painters reached one of their highest points as artists.

After Peisistratus died in 527 BCE, his sons Hippias and Hipparchus took over as tyrants. But the Athenians were starting to resent the absolute rule of the Peisistratus family, and in 514 BCE, Hipparchus was assassinated by two men named Harmodius and Aristogiton. The two tyrannicides were declared heroes. A popular song celebrated their action:

A popular Athenian song, about 514 BCE

> I will carry my sword in a bough of myrtle
> Just as Harmodius and Aristogiton did
> When they killed the tyrants.
> And put Athens on a just footing.

Hippias was forced to flee Athens a few years later.

As an Englishman said more than 2,000 years after the rise of the Greek tyrants, "Power tends to corrupt and absolute power corrupts absolutely." It is very tempting for someone who isn't governed by any laws to get a little relaxed about the difference between right and wrong. Some Greeks resented these absolute rulers and the word *tyrannos* took on the negative meaning that "tyrant" has today.

But oddly, the tyranny of Peisistratus proved to be a first step toward democracy, or government by the people. During his rule, elections continued to be held (although the tyrant's friends got elected in suspiciously large numbers) and juries kept hearing cases. So once Peisistratus and his sons were gone, the Athenians were able to take the next steps toward full democracy.

It was as a prosperous democracy that Athens entered the fifth century BCE. The Athenians would need prosperity and a strong government to face the challenges ahead of them.

MEANWHILE IN SOUTH ASIA . . .

Prosperity wasn't important to everyone in the ancient world. Born in the Kosala kingdom, near the border of modern Nepal and India, Prince Gautama was raised in luxury. He grew disturbed at the thought of illness, old age, and death, and left his wife and son to search for truth and the meaning of life. By fasting, meditating, and living simply, he reached the understanding he was seeking.

He became known as the Buddha, or enlightened one, and encouraged his followers to find peace by rejecting material comforts. The belief system known as Buddhism, based on the Buddha's teachings, spread from India to the rest of Asia and is now practiced all over the world.

Harmodius and Aristogiton assassinated the tyrant Hipparchus in 514 BCE. Harmodius (right) was killed during the assassination, and Aristogiton (left) was captured and tortured to death.

CHAPTER 9

"A LIVING POSSESSION"
SLAVERY

CRATES,
XENOPHON, AND
ARISTOTLE

It's hard for a modern person to imagine how much hard work ancient people had to do just to stay alive. About 80 percent of all Greek workers were involved in agriculture. Greeks who had their own land looked down on people who farmed someone else's land for pay, or made the useful clay pots, or hammered out the armor that soldiers needed.

Many upper-class Greeks mistrusted and disliked the laborers. It would be easy for us to think that these Athenians were ungrateful people who sneered at the workers who made their city wealthy and powerful. But most people, probably including the laborers themselves, thought that the gods put people in the position they were supposed to be in. If you were a bricklayer, it was because you were meant to be a bricklayer. If you could be useful being a sailor, then you had to be a sailor. By this reasoning, putting a sailor into a general's position would be like using a lawnmower to wash your dishes or using a computer as a paperweight.

And if you were meant to be a slave, the gods made you a slave. Slavery was common throughout the ancient world. No one knows exactly when people started enslaving each other, although the practice started long before recorded history. This is certainly true in Greece. Documents

Both slaves and free people farmed the land. This sculpture shows a farmer plowing with his team of cattle.

from the very early civilization of Mycenae show a large number of slaves, many of them working for the *wanax,* or ruler.

This is not to say that everybody in ancient Greece thought that owning another human being was a good thing. In a play called *The Beasts,* written by the fifth-century BCE playwright Crates, one of the characters tells his friend about an ideal world he's dreamed up in which nobody is allowed to have a slave:

> Everything will come to people as soon as they call for it. "Table, put yourself down right here next to me. . . . Fill up, jug. . . . Get moving, fish!" "But I'm not toasted on the other side yet!" "Well then, why don't you turn yourself over—and cover yourself with oil and salt while you're at it!"

But in reality, a high percentage of the ancient Greek population was made up of enslaved people, especially after the sixth century BCE. Some historians think that of the roughly 250,000 people in Attica, the territory of Athens, about 80,000 to 100,000 were enslaved.

We know much less about enslaved people than we do about free people. The Greeks kept very few records about slaves, so historians have a hard time figuring out some of the details about their lives.

Many slaves were foreigners who had been captured in wars or by pirates who seized sailors as well as their cargo. Since Greeks mostly looked down on people from other countries, they thought that it was only natural for these "inferior" people to be enslaved.

Sometimes Greeks enslaved other Greeks, although they preferred not to. In a long war between Athens and Sparta, the Athenians were sometimes so angry and frustrated that they would enslave the entire populations of cities that weren't fighting on their side. Criminals might be condemned to enslavement. Also, some people's desperate poverty forced them to sell themselves or their children. People who owed a lot of money might wind up paying off their debt with themselves, in place of the cash they didn't have. This

66 Crates, *The Beasts,* mid-fifth century BCE

Who Is a Citizen?

Some Greek states did not allow manual laborers to vote. The philosopher Aristotle sounds like a modern-day snob:

"*There were some states, in the earliest times, where the class of laborers was actually composed of slaves or foreigners exclusively, which explains why so many laborers are slaves or foreigners even today. The best form of the state will not make the laborer a citizen.*"

Slaves wore tattoos to indicate where they came from. The tattoos on the arms and neck of this slave show that she is from Thrace, not from Greece.

setup could be temporary, with the person eventually working off the debt. Children of slaves were also slaves.

Slaves were looked on as tools, just like a computer or a chainsaw today. A few extremely wealthy people lived off the labor of their slaves. But many people who owned slaves also worked, just as many people today who own computers and chainsaws work. Another way to profit was to rent slaves out to other people who needed their labor for only a short period, such as during planting or harvest time. Cities and towns might own slaves who did public work such as street repair and construction.

Of course, most slaves worked harder than most free people. And some of the slaves' jobs were terribly dangerous and degrading. One of the worst fates was to be sent to the silver mines, where thousands of slaves died of overwork and accidents. Farm slaves also had hard (and usually short) lives. Some oarsmen on warships were slaves, although others were highly trained sailors.

Sometimes slaves were semi-independent. Craftsmen set up slaves in workshops and took a portion of what the slave earned by metalworking, pottery, tailoring, and other crafts. The slave could often keep the rest.

At least one slave managed to do even better than that. His name was Pasion, and he worked for two bankers in Athens's port city of Piraeus. He did such a good job and learned so much that the bankers freed him, and he started

"A slave is a living possession."
—Aristotle, *Politics*, mid-fourth century BCE

his own business. He set up shop in Athens as a banker, and also started a shield-making business. He became the wealthiest banker and manufacturer of his time in the area.

Pasion was a loyal member of his adopted *polis*, and made many charitable contributions to Athens. In return, the *polis* made him and his descendants Athenian citizens. His spending habits caught up with him, though: when he died, he owed more money than he left to his heirs.

Pasion was an exception. Most slaves spent their entire lives without the hope of freedom, and very few of them were entrusted with such important and complicated work as banking.

Many of them worked in the household. They could be cooks, maids, gardeners, companions, and occasionally tutors to their masters' children. Female slaves performed many of the traditional women's jobs in the home such as weaving and cooking, sometimes alongside the free women, sometimes taking over the more difficult parts of the task.

If they were well educated, slaves might be assigned specialized work, such as copying books. Talented women might do fine needlework. Slaves also often took care of babies and small children.

Many people today would feel uncomfortable if the people protecting them and their property had lost their freedom. Apparently some Greeks were fine with this, because the police forces in many *poleis* were made up, at least in part, of slaves. When states were really worried about losing a war, they would

One way to buy freedom was for a slave to deposit money in an account at a religious site. The owner would then "sell" the slave to the god and take the money from that account. This wall at the city of Delphi records some of these transactions.

The Ants and the Grasshopper

Aesop was a Greek slave who wrote fables. This one may be familiar, although nowadays, storytellers sometimes change the ending to make the ants take pity on the grasshopper:

"*The ants were spending a beautiful winter day drying the grain they had collected in the summer. A grasshopper, desperately hungry, passed by and earnestly begged for a little food. When the ants asked him why he hadn't stored food up during the summer, he said, 'I had no time. I spent my days singing.' The ants laughed at him. 'If you were so foolish as to sing the summer away,' they said, 'then you must dance supperless to bed now that winter has come.'*"

66 Xenophon, *On Household Management,* early fourth century BCE

sometimes have slaves serve in the military. Most school-teachers were also slaves, as were many doctors.

The lives of these more privileged slaves were usually not as hard as those of agricultural workers or slaves who worked in mines. But nothing could change the fact that they were enslaved. They were owned in the same way that a chair or a horse was owned. If a slave was injured, the person whose fault it was had to pay a fine to the owner—not to the injured person. In fact, their only rights were that they couldn't be killed and the only person who could hit them was their owner.

Slaves could not participate in many religious sects. Religion was important to the Greeks, so this must have been a real hardship. And a law said that the only way a slave's evidence could be used in court would be if it was obtained under torture. It appears, however, that this method of getting evidence was rarely (if ever) used.

Generally, people were enslaved for life, but there were some exceptions. Occasionally a childless couple would adopt a young slave and raise the child as their own. Sometimes an owner would free a slave (who usually had to keep performing some service for the former owner) and sometimes slaves were freed in the owner's will. At times a really heartless slave-owner would free slaves who had become old or sick. It was cheaper than having to support them.

The historian Xenophon thought up a reward system to make his slaves work harder and seemed to recognize that they were human. He wrote in his book *On Household Management:*

> I . . . reward the better worker with better clothing and shoes and give the worse clothing and shoes to the worse worker. Slaves get very discouraged if they see that they're doing all the work but the others get the same rewards. I personally think that better slaves should not be treated in the same way as worse ones.

But at times he also compares them to animals

> It's possible to make human beings more disposed to obey merely by explaining to them the advantages of

obedience, but things are different with slaves. With slaves, the training considered appropriate to wild animals is a particularly useful method of instilling obedience.

Greeks worried about slave revolts. Both Plato and Aristotle said that it was a good idea not to have all the slaves in the house come from the same part of the world and speak the same language. This would reduce the risk of a revolt or other problems for the owner. But it also must have made life very lonely for the slaves, who were forced to live among people with a different language and much different culture from their own.

It was very rare for slaves to gain freedom by running away. Where would they run to, after all? Slavery was legal everywhere they could go.

How could the same society make slaves teachers and doctors and also compare them to animals, without the ability to reason? In his *Politics* the philosopher Aristotle wrote that

> The rule of the free over the slave is of one nature; that of the male over the female another; and that of the adult over the child another still. The slave utterly lacks the capacity for thinking; the female has it, but in an ill-defined form; and if children have it too, it is only in an immature form.

Yet he freed several slaves in his will. Did he think they would suddenly become smart the day he died? Or did he think that there was something about being enslaved that took away the ability to reason? If that was the case, wouldn't he be making society better by freeing as many slaves as possible, or even campaigning to abolish the practice? Then you would have many more thinking, reasoning people to participate in the community.

But that didn't happen. Life was good in Athens, as long as you were a free adult male. Slaves, women, and children enjoyed some great benefits from living in Athens, but only as second- (or third- or fourth-) class citizens.

66 Aristotle, *Politics*, mid-fourth century BCE

CHAPTER 10

GROWING UP GREEK
GREEK CHILDHOOD

Being young in ancient Greece was a risky proposition. Some historians think that about one-third of all babies died before their first birthday, and some parents must have tried hard not to get too attached to their children until it looked like they were going to survive. Once they seemed reasonably sure of living to grow up, children started going to school, playing, and learning how to be good citizens.

School, play, citizenship—growing up in Greece, once the dangers of babyhood were past—might sound similar to growing up today. Actually, a lot has changed since then, sometimes for the better and sometimes for the worse.

You probably spend most of your day at school. That's one big change. Many fewer young people in ancient Greece went to school and the ones who did were mostly boys. They came from the better-off families. Some girls were taught to read and write, but that was unusual.

In the relief sculpture on this grave monument, parents mourn the death of their daughter, who is clasping her mother's hand in farewell.

If you weren't one of the lucky few to get an education, you probably spent most of your waking hours at work. The most common work in ancient Greece was farming, and even very small children were useful on a farm.

If the family business was to make cooking pots, or shoes, or bricks, boys probably had to start helping out as soon as they were old enough to understand what to do and were strong enough to do it. Girls learned to spin and weave very early.

Historians don't know much about the lives of ordinary Greek people like farmers and brick-makers, and even less about the lives of their children. This means that it's almost impossible to find out anything about children except a few from the best-educated and wealthiest families. We can get an idea, though, that even for them it wasn't all rosy. The philosopher Aristotle, who was from one of those wealthy families, says in his *Eudemian Ethics*, "the kind of life people lead when they're still children is not desirable; as a matter of fact, nobody in his right mind could bear to return to that time of life."

Another difficulty in learning about family life in ancient Greece is that a lot of our information comes from people who are writing about what life *should* be like. That's not the best place to find out about their reality.

However, if everyone is leading their lives exactly the way they're supposed to, it is a waste of time to tell them how they should act. So if you find a lot of advice about how to behave, you can bet that at least some people aren't doing what the writers think they ought to do, or they would have found something else to write about.

Take relationships between husbands and wives, for example. In most Greek marriages, the husband was much older than his wife. Many Athenian girls got married when they were the same age as the average ninth grader today. But a man had to be able to support a family, so unless he inherited a fortune from his family, he was likely to be 30 years old or so by the time he had enough money to get married. A teenage girl could suddenly go from being the daughter of the house one day to being the person running

66 Aristotle, *Eudemian Ethics*, mid-fourth century BCE

This fourth-century BCE doll was found at the sanctuary of Demeter and Persephone, mother and daughter goddesses, in the city of Corinth. It may have been an offering or toy.

💬 Plato, *Meno*, early fourth century BCE

an entire household the next day. An inscription made to commemorate the marriage of a girl shows how fast she had to grow up. It says that she dedicated to Artemis "her tambourine, her pretty ball and the net that upheld her hair, her dolls too, and their dresses" right before becoming a wife. Wives' roles were clearly defined. The philosopher Plato wrote in the *Meno* that a friend of Socrates said,

> If you want a definition of virtue in a man, that's easy to find: virtue for a man is the ability to conduct the city's affairs in such a way as to help his friends, hurt his enemies, and see to it that he avoids being hurt himself. If you want a definition of virtue in a woman, that's not hard to describe: she must run the household well, looking after everything that it contains, and obey her husband.

There were of course some families where the wife and husband didn't behave exactly in that way. If everyone acted the same, male and female roles would have been so obvious that Plato wouldn't have had to define them. The real and the ideal most likely weren't always the same.

Another aspect of the ideal family was that the women and children spent their days in a separate part of the house from the men, usually with servants or slaves. They even took their meals separately, especially when the men invited friends to dinner. Women were so hidden, in fact, that in upper-class homes they weren't even supposed to go outside. Instead, the men and the slaves did the shopping and the other errands.

This means that the ideal family was also rich—not many average people could afford a large staff of slaves and separate living quarters for them. And not many families could survive if only the man supported it financially.

People who wrote about the ideal family hardly ever mention disease and death. But the cold, hard facts tell us that many Greek children died young. Without modern medicines, vaccinations, and sanitation, illnesses that hardly make you sick today, or that people don't even get any more, could wipe out whole families at once. Babies were especially vulnerable.

If the parents were too poor to raise a child, or if a newborn had a handicap, sometimes a decision would be made to expose the baby. This meant leaving the child somewhere outside away from home, all alone. Historians know this wasn't against the law, but they don't know if it was a common practice. Surely some parents hoped that the baby would be found and raised by another family, but they must have known that the child would probably die. Sometimes exposed babies would be found and raised as slaves.

If the parents took this drastic step, they could either try again for a healthy child or might be better able to support their children who had already survived the most difficult part of life—the first few months after birth. After living past infancy, a child was a part of the family. Children who died were mourned as much as adults were. An epitaph for one little girl reads:

> Often in lamentation upon this girl's tomb her mother Cleina
> Bewails her beloved child who dies before her time.

Poor diet might have had a lot to do with early deaths. Not all mothers breast-fed their babies. Baby bottles had not been invented yet, so some wealthy families hired a woman to breast-feed the baby. Sometimes this nurse wasn't well nourished and couldn't provide enough milk. And when the surviving children were old enough to eat food, it was sometimes difficult to get the right kind of nutrition from the foods that were available.

Greece is a warm country, and it was hard to preserve food. Protein was hard to come by. You'd think that in a

NASTY, BRUTISH, AND SHORT

The life expectancy of an ancient Greek who made it past childhood illnesses was about 36 years for women and 45 years for men. The difference is explained by the better nutrition boys received and by the fact that childbirth was very dangerous for both mother and infant in those days.

❝ Epitaph for a little girl, about 200 BCE

country surrounded by the sea, the Greeks would have eaten a lot of fish, but for some reason they didn't. Meat was expensive and many times people were limited to eating the leftovers of animals sacrificed to the gods. Rich and poor, they lived mostly on vegetables, cheese, grains, and olives. During the winter or when the harvest was bad, famines would kill great numbers of people. Many of the survivors would be so weakened that they would later die of an illness that normally wasn't dangerous.

Everybody drank wine mixed with water, even the children. If they had dessert, it probably would be fruit (when they could afford it or grow it themselves) or grain sweetened with honey.

But there were many good things about growing up Greek. In most of Greece, you can expect good weather much of the time. Playing outdoors must have been fun, with warm water to wade and swim in and lots of hills and valleys to explore. Greek children could play ball games and had simple toys like yo-yos and clay animals on wheels that could be pulled with a string. There were some board games, mostly played with dice and counters.

On many religious holidays there would be parties and special food. Some people wouldn't have to work (but farmers never really get a day off) and families would get together to celebrate.

Was Aristotle right about the misery of a Greek childhood? Or were there enough good times to make up for the problems? Unfortunately, if any Greek child wrote a diary or any other record of his or her life, it hasn't survived, so all we can do is guess.

Although the game depicted on this statue-base looks very similar to hockey, no descriptions of how it was played have survived.

CHAPTER 11

"A SHADOWY EXISTENCE"
THE WOMEN OF ANCIENT GREECE

❝ EURIPIDES, PLATO, HOMER, HESIOD, SEMONIDES, XENOPHON, AND PHINTYS

Is this fair? A whole separate chapter on women? Where's the chapter on men? Why do women get special treatment?

Actually, it's the men, not the women, who are getting special treatment. In the rest of this book, you can read about an awful lot of men but not many women. Since they're hardly mentioned in history books, some people wrongly assume that ancient Greek women must not have been very important.

The problem is that nobody knows precisely how women lived and what they did in ancient Greece. Historians pick and choose what they put into their books and few ancient Greek historians chose to include women very often. Herodotus mentioned women and even girls, but he was unusual.

Thucydides, on the other hand, was mainly interested in the kind of history that records warfare and diplomacy. And even though we don't know much about Greek women, we do know that they had very small parts to play in those areas of life. They couldn't hold office in most ancient Greek governments and they weren't allowed to be soldiers. The important work that women did at home to keep things going—farming, supervising households, raising families, everything they took care of in peacetime plus assuming the jobs customarily done by men in times of war—wasn't the focus of his histories. So Thucydides rarely mentioned women.

The playwright Euripides assumed there was friendship and support between women when he had one of his characters in *Iphigenia Among the Taurians* say, "Women we are, each other's steadfast friends, Allies whenever common needs arise."

TAKE THAT!

Not only was it rare for a woman to be in charge, but it was also unusual for one to fight in a war. Queen Artemisia of Halicarnassus did both, siding with the enemy Persians against other Greeks. Artemisia commanded a war ship and a reward was offered for her capture.

One Greek ship came close to collecting the money. But Artemisia tricked them by ordering her sailors to make her ship turn and ram a Persian ship. The Greeks figured that they must have been mistaken and that the ship they were chasing must not be Artemisia's. Why would she attack someone on her own side? So they sailed away to look for her somewhere else and she escaped.

❝ Euripides, *Iphigenia Among the Taurians*, about 413 BCE

Plato, *Laws*, mid-fourth century BCE

The philosopher Plato showed some sympathy for their lives when he said in the *Laws* that women were "accustomed to a confined and shadowy existence."

Even by the time the very early poet Homer was writing, women had fairly defined roles. Or at least they were supposed to. Penelope, who waited for many years for her husband Odysseus to return from the Trojan War, wanted to get rid of the men who had been trying to force her to marry one of them. But her own son Telemachus wouldn't let her do anything about it. According to Homer, Telemachus said in the *Odyssey*,

Homer, *Odyssey*, about 725 BCE

> Go therefore back in the house, and take up your
>   own work,
> The loom and the distaff, and see to it that your
>   handmaidens
> Ply their work also; but the men must see to discussion,
> All men, but I most of all. For mine is the power in
>   this household.

But in another part of the *Odyssey*, Homer shows us that maybe all houses weren't run that way. A princess tells Odysseus:

> Go on quickly across the hall until you come to
> My mother, and she will be sitting beside the hearth,
>   in the firelight, . . .
> And there is my father's chair of state, drawn close
>   beside her. . . .
> Go on past him and then with your arms embrace
>   our mother's
> Knees; do this, and you will behold your day of
>   homecoming
> With happiness and speed, even if you live very far off.

So in this house, anyway, the father just *thought* he was running the show.

Penelope was everything the Greeks believed a woman should be: loyal to her husband, a good daughter in law, dedicated to running her house well, spending most of her time spinning and weaving, never going outdoors. But

Homer also shows another kind of woman: Clytemnestra, the wife of King Agamemnon, was unfaithful to her husband and then killed him. Unfortunately, Homer said in the *Odyssey*, Penelope's goodness doesn't help women's reputation. All it shows is that one woman was good. Clytemnestra's wickedness, however, makes *all* women look bad:

> [A] song of loathing
> Will be hers among men, to make evil the reputation
> Of womankind, even for those whose acts are virtuous.

66 Homer, *Odyssey*, about 725 BCE

But Homer was unusual in recognizing that some women were virtuous. Most Greek writers had many nasty things to say about women and they didn't often bother to find the exceptions to their negative images. Hesiod, who lived at about the same time as Homer, had much to say about Pandora, the woman who, according to Greek mythology, brought evil into the world. Zeus sent her to punish men because he was angry at them. Hesiod says she was a "sheer inescapable snare for men" and since she was the mother of all women, they are all just as bad as she was. He says that women are "a great plague" and "an evil for men."

66 Hesiod, *The Theogony*, around 700 BCE

It's sometimes hard to know if a poet means what he says, or is just exaggerating to make a point. It is also hard to take a writer seriously when he claims something totally ridiculous. The poet Semonides said that one kind of woman descends from pigs and you can tell this because she leaves her house in a mess. Another woman is the

Many women were involved in the important task of making cloth. Large looms, like the one depicted on this vase, required skillful hands working together.

AMAZONS

The Amazons were supposed to be a tribe of warrior women who lived apart from men. Many people think they never existed. In 1997, however, archaeologists found some burial mounds in Russia that seem to indicate that wandering groups of women rode horses and fought with arrows. It's possible that tales of these women inspired the stories of Amazons told by the Greeks.

Xenophon, *The Spartan Constitution*, early fourth century BCE

Atalanta, shown on this vase, defied tradition by refusing to marry. When her father told her that she had to find a husband, she said that she would marry a man who could beat her in a race. Aphrodite, the goddess of love, helped a man trick her into losing.

great-granddaughter of the mischievous fox, who gets into trouble through her nosiness. Still another must have a donkey for an ancestor, because she's so stubborn and loves to eat. Only the woman who descends from the bee—hard working, humble, neat, with lots of children—seems to be worth marrying. The Greeks had some ideas about natural history that seem very odd to us today but surely nobody, even at that time, believed that all this was true. It's so silly that Semonides was probably joking.

One thing most ancient Greek writers seem to have agreed upon is that the reason there are women is so that there can be children. Women seem to have had very little worth in many writers' eyes, except for that one function. The historian Xenophon wrote in *The Spartan Constitution* that except in Sparta "girls destined for motherhood and who are considered to be well brought up subsist on the most basic diet and are allowed a minimum of delicacies." Why do they need good nutrition, after all? It's not as if they're going to do anything hard, like plowing a field. (The Greeks had no idea how important it is for pregnant women to eat well.)

Have you noticed anything about who wrote all these plays, poems, and histories? They're all men. Actually, that's true in most other chapters, too. This doesn't mean that women would necessarily have said anything nicer about themselves than men did. But it's clear we're not getting a well-rounded view of how women lived in ancient Greece. The female poet Sappho wrote some poems about individual women, but it's hard to find out much about women in general from them, except that some women were well-enough educated to write exceptionally beautiful poems. Some upper-class women were educated, but we'll probably never know how many of them could read and write (we don't know that about men, either). They certainly weren't expected to work outside the home, so their education was not for job training.

So what do we know for sure from the women themselves? Precious little. We do have an essay *On the Proper Behavior for Wives* that was probably written by a Greek woman named Phintys, who saw basic differences between men and women:

> I agree that men should be generals and city officials and politicians, and women should keep house and stay inside and receive and take care of their husbands. But I believe that courage, justice, and intelligence are qualities that men and women have in common. . . . Courage and intelligence are more appropriately male qualities because of the strength of men's bodies and the power of their minds. Chastity is more appropriately female.

In general, females were not valued as highly as males in ancient Greece. Aside from not being given as much to eat, as Xenophon mentioned, girls were probably not as well taken care of in other ways, too. Lists of citizens, gravestones, and other kinds of evidence show many more adult males than females, which suggests that many girls died as babies and toddlers.

Many people, naturally, loved their little girls and even took their advice. King Cleomenes of Sparta allowed his daughter Gorgo to sit in on a conversation with Aristagoras, the tyrant of the *polis* of Miletus, when she was about eight years old. After listening to the Milesian's offers of money if

Continues on page 80

MEANWHILE IN CHINA . . .

In ancient China, women rarely had political power, and married women were taught that their husbands ruled over them. Few women learned to read and write. One exception was Ban Zhao, who wrote a history of the ruling family of China in the first or second century CE. This text became a model for histories written by Chinese scholars who came after her. She also was the author of a *Lessons for Women,* a manual instructing women how to behave.

Phintys, *On the Proper Behavior for Wives,* about 200 BCE

ARCHAEOLOGIST AT WORK:
AN INTERVIEW WITH BARBARA TSAKIRGIS

Professor Barbara Tsakirgis is an archaeologist who excavates ancient houses in Athens and in Greek Sicily, and studies how people lived in them. She teaches classics and art history at Vanderbilt University.

What's different about excavating a temple and a house?

The techniques are the same, but honestly, the expectations are quite different. Most houses are built in a much more modest fashion, as you'd expect if you were to compare a modern house with a church, say, or with a courthouse. The temples were made of large blocks of stone, but the houses were built with very low stone bases to the walls, and the rest was made of mud brick. What's also different are the things that you find inside. In general, Greek temples didn't have much inside. What was inside was extraordinarily valuable and long since taken away. Houses have, in some instances, a vast amount of stuff in them. They might have pots and pans, they might have loom weights used by the women of the house who wove wool or linen. They might have braziers—little charcoal burners that they used in heating and cooking and for light.

Did you ever find anything that surprised you?

It's usually the case that ancient cities were abandoned, and the people would take with them anything of value. On occasion, the pieces that are left behind are very puzzling. One large object found in a house looks for all the world like a chimney pot. But there is a great deal of debate over whether Greek houses had chimneys. So either it came from a very unusual house, or we have to revise our view of Greek chimneys.

Have you ever found human remains?

I haven't myself dug where there were human remains, but they have occasionally appeared in houses. In one of our houses in Sicily, the excavator found a human skeleton in a cistern, a water storage tank. And we have no idea how that person ended up in the cistern. It's certainly not a place where people are buried, certainly not within a house.

And certainly not if you're going to drink water out of the cistern! So when you find something unusual, do you call in an expert? Do they call in a forensic scientist to find out if the person was murdered, for example?

Absolutely. There's a whole class of archaeologists who deal with human bone remains, and they can tell all sorts of things from the bones. By careful examination, all sorts of evidence can be read from the human bones. We had one person in the excavation in Athens who deals with the bones from a number of graves from the Byzantine era, the Greek Middle Ages. She showed me this most horrific part of a jaw, which was the best advertisement I've ever seen for going to the dentist regularly. It was a jawbone with literally a hole through it. What she thought was the case was that the person had a cavity or some kind of infection in the tooth that developed into an abscess in a period, of course, long before antibiotics, and the tooth was not pulled. Eventually the infection ate through the tooth, through the jawbone, and then erupted into the brain cavity where undoubtedly the infection killed the person.

It's horrifying but it's fascinating. When I look at bones, I just see bones. But when these bone people look at bones, they show you these delicate little holes through which the nerves were strung, they can show you the points of attachment for the various connective tissues. They can, in some cases, tell you the gender of the individual, the age, the quality of nutrition.

Do you ever find artworks?
One of the most attractive aspects of the ancient Greek houses are the floors. Often in one or two rooms, especially the dining room, there will be a mosaic floor, made up of pebbles, and later of little cubes of stone. Sometimes they show mythological scenes, and sometimes they're just decorative borders with animals and flowers. And I have to say that many of these mosaics are quite beautiful.

They preserve quite well, but unfortunately they're extremely difficult to excavate. In one case in Morgantina (a city in Sicily that was once a Greek colony), the figure is made up of really quite minute pieces of stone, some of which are only a millimeter on a side. If the soil is loose, if there have been trees or plants allowed to grow around a mosaic like that, even the most delicate roots can dislodge the tesserae (small, usually four-sided pieces of glass, stone, or tile used to make a mosaic).

So do you have to remove it in one huge piece?
Well, it's a very time-consuming process to excavate a mosaic, and generally you have to use very delicate tools. The tool that dentists use to clean the spaces between your teeth is one of our favorite tools to use in cases like this.

If a mosaic has to be moved for its own safety or to be restored, it's usually taken up in sections. The way that's done is that a reversible glue is spread over the top of the mosaic or a part of it, and then a mesh sheet is laid over that. And then that rectangle or square that has been covered is literally cut from the rest of the mosaic. The sheet adheres to the face of the mosaic and then you can lift it up. There's often a great deal of damage to the edge where the cut is.

I bet the pieces are heavy.
They are very heavy, and it's very labor-intensive work. A friend of mine digging a Roman bath mosaic said that the removal process took over a year.

When you remove something like that, do you restore it on-site or do you send it to somebody?
Most large excavations will hire a conservator to work on-site. Conservators are hard to come by, and they're very expensive. They have to go to school for seven years. There's chemistry involved, there's art history, there's a lot that goes into it.

Women's lives were so controlled that when they had the chance to be free, they sometimes went wild. This dancing maenad, or worshiper of the god Dionysus, carries a staff called a thyrsus in her right hand and a dead leopard in her left.

Continued from page 77

Cleomenes would do what he wanted, Gorgo cried out, "Father, this stranger will corrupt you if you do not leave at once." Cleomenes followed her advice and never did make an alliance with Aristagoras. The Milesian must have been astonished that the king would follow the advice of a child, especially a female.

What would a woman do all day? In most periods of Greek history, upper-class women were supposed to stay indoors all the time. They didn't even go out to do the shopping, but sent their servants and slaves to the market instead. (Some of these servants were women, but since they weren't from the upper classes, no one seemed to care that they were exposed to all the roughness of the outside world.) Instead, the women were in charge of running the household, and they did the spinning and weaving that provided the clothes, sheets, and everything else made of cloth that the family needed. They must have looked forward to religious festivals, where they would get to see the town and mingle with other people.

Many women had to work, of course. They farmed and made crafts and played music and danced. A few served as priestesses to goddesses. And there was one job for which women were considered ideal: being a professional mourner. When a wealthy person died, women were hired to weep and carry on at the funeral so that everyone would be impressed at how beloved the dead person was. No one seemed to find it odd that the people making a big fuss over someone's death weren't his friends or relatives, but someone paid to cry. Most women in Greece led lives that look very restricted to many of us today. This makes the achievements of the women who did manage to contribute to their society even more remarkable.

MAENADS

Women rarely managed to break free of their restricted lives. But female followers of the god Dionysus held rituals where they would go into ecstasies. (The word comes from *ek-stasis*, which means "standing outside yourself.") In one myth, they tore a young man limb from limb because he said he didn't believe in Dionysus.

CHAPTER 12

THE SPARTAN EXPERIMENT

DAILY LIFE IN ANCIENT SPARTA

❝ XENOPHON,
PLUTARCH,
HERODOTUS, AND
MENANDER

You might have heard someone say that so-and-so lives a "Spartan existence." This means that so-and-so doesn't own many nice things, doesn't eat out much, and wears plain clothes. But the real people who lived in the *polis* of Sparta deprived themselves of a lot more than luxuries—and were proud of it.

Imagine you are a twelve-year-old Spartan girl in the sixth century BCE. You live with your mother, your sisters, and your little brothers. You have a father, but you hardly ever see him. In fact, you hardly ever see any men, or even any boys near your age. When your brother turned seven, he was taken away. You missed him at first, but for his whole life you knew that this would happen some day, so you quickly got over it.

Most Greek cities were built on hilltops to make them easier to defend from attackers. The Spartans built their city on a plain to tell potential attackers that they were so powerful that they didn't need a hill to protect them.

This statue of a Spartan racing girl shows the kind of clothing other Greeks called "phainomerides"—thigh displayers!

Your days are very busy. Unlike most Greek girls, you don't have to worry too much about learning how to spin yarn and weave cloth. Instead, you have to run and do other exercises to get strong. Your exercise skirt is so short that a girl from any other part of Greece would be punished for wearing it. Sometimes you work out naked, which shocks the other Greeks.

You are constantly told to be strong. But this isn't because people care about your health. It's because strong girls grow up to be strong women, and strong women—everyone tells you—have healthy sons. And sons are important. Sons grow up to be warriors and leaders.

Now imagine you're that girl's younger brother. For your whole life, you've been spoiled by your mother and your sisters, who were proud to have such a healthy boy in the family. You always knew that when you turned seven, you would be taken away to live with your father and the other men—away from the weakening influence of all those women—so you were excited when the big day finally came.

But life with the men isn't as much fun as you thought it would be. Instead of being everyone's pampered pet, you are toughened up. You're always kept a little hungry. That way, you'll think of clever ways to steal food. And although you get punished if you're caught, the punishment is not for stealing, but for being careless enough to get caught.

WELL, YOU ASKED!

Probably some Spartan mothers grieved for their children who were taken away from them. But many were proud of the strength of their sons and contemptuous of the children of other Greek women. When an Athenian woman asked Sparta's Queen Gorgo, "Why is it that you Spartan women are the only ones who can rule men?" Gorgo replied, "Because we are the only ones who give birth to men."

You wrestle, run, and do other exercises to strengthen your muscles. Every day you have to swim in the ice-cold Eurotas River. You are frequently beaten, often for no reason. The older boys and the men tell you that this will make you even stronger.

And what is all this hard work for? It's to make you into a soldier. Not just any soldier, but a Spartan soldier, a member of one of the toughest, most feared armies the world has ever known.

The Spartan way of life is hard for us to understand because many practices that most of us take for granted were done in exactly the opposite way there. In the United States, the government is "of the people, by the people, for the people." But in Sparta, the state did not exist for the people—the people existed for the state.

Ants in an anthill die without hesitation to preserve the queen and the health of the colony. The individual ant counts for nothing. The situation was the same in Sparta. It was a great honor to die for Sparta because one's death would benefit the Spartans as a whole. The greatest shame was to run from danger. The Athenian historian Xenophon wrote in his *Hellenica* that after a battle in 371 BCE, when the Spartans were badly beaten,

> Those whose relatives had been killed could be seen going around in public looking cheerful and serene, but on the whole those whose relatives were reported to have survived kept to themselves, and those of them who did venture out were seen walking around looking very glum and even sorry for themselves.

Spartan society was structured much differently from the rest of the Greek world. First of all, it was divided into three classes. The *helots*, or slaves, did the heavy work of farming. They had even lower status than that of slaves in the rest of Greece, and could even be killed for no reason. They were beaten once a year as a reminder of their enslavement.

Above the helots were the *perioeci*, or "neighbors." They were not slaves, but were not fully citizens, since they could

SPARTA, 600 BCE

" Xenophon, *Hellenica*, mid-fourth century BCE

Bronze armor was relatively light and very strong. In addition to the pieces shown here, warriors often wore shin-guards and carried shields.

A Patriotic Poet

Most of the poems written by the few Spartan poets have been lost. It's no surprise that poems about war were the favorites of Spartan poets. Here is part of an untitled poem by Tyrtaeus:

"It is a good thing to lose your life fighting in the front ranks, Giving your life for father, city, people. . . . The glory of a man like this is not forgotten; His name remembered, he becomes eternal."

not vote. The *perioeci* did metal-work, made pots, spun wool, wove clothing—did most of the day-to-day work besides farming, in fact.

The highest class of people was called "The Equals." The name didn't mean that they were equal to the other groups, but that they were equal to each other. Their job was to protect Sparta at all cost. There were never more than 9,000 "Equals" (all of them men), and they were the only Spartans who could vote.

Many Greek *poleis* were at war much of the time, and even in peace, war always threatened. So most Greek men were ready to quit living their regular lives and become soldiers when necessary. But the Spartans went further. They were so concerned about war that they decided to organize their entire society around the military and created a whole class of people whose only purpose was to protect the state.

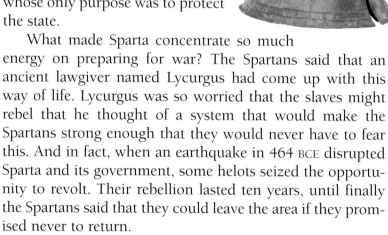

What made Sparta concentrate so much energy on preparing for war? The Spartans said that an ancient lawgiver named Lycurgus had come up with this way of life. Lycurgus was so worried that the slaves might rebel that he thought of a system that would make the Spartans strong enough that they would never have to fear this. And in fact, when an earthquake in 464 BCE disrupted Sparta and its government, some helots seized the opportunity to revolt. Their rebellion lasted ten years, until finally the Spartans said that they could leave the area if they promised never to return.

So, concern over the threat by their neighbors and fear of the large numbers of helots living among them led the Spartan ruling class to concentrate their energy on strength.

Part of what the Spartans saw as strength was a reliance on men to run things. Spartan women were not included in the government at all. But they were as fiercely patriotic as the men. Mothers, wives, and sisters encouraged the men to fight and were proud when they died. In his *Sayings of the Spartan Women,* the biographer and essayist Plutarch reports two episodes that demonstrate their attitude:

> A mother was burying her son when an ordinary old woman came up to her and said, "Oh, you poor thing. What terrible luck!" "No, by the gods," she replied, "it is good luck, for I brought him into the world so that he might die for Sparta, and this is the very thing that has happened."

> One woman, seeing her son coming towards her after a battle, asked him how things had gone for Sparta. When he said, "Everyone has perished," she picked up a tile and hurled it at him, killing him, saying, "And so you're the one they picked to bring the bad news?"

" Plutarch, *Sayings of the Spartan Women,* about 100 CE

The other Greeks had a kind of love-hate relationship with the Spartans. The Athenians admired the toughness of Spartan children so much that sometimes they would hire Spartan nursemaids for their own children. They were also envious of the stability of the Spartan government.

The Spartans held on to the **monarchy** long after most other Greek *poleis* had decided to be ruled by elected officials. In order to keep any one man from becoming too powerful, Sparta had two kings at a time. One king was in charge of the army, and the other governed matters at home. They shared responsibility for religious duties.

monos + archon = "one" + "ruler" "Monarchy" means "government by a single ruler."

The Spartan kings did not have absolute power, but were members of the Council of Elders, called the Gerousia. The other 28 Elders were elected, and while any man over the age of 60 was eligible, the Elders were usually wealthy aristocrats. In addition to the Elders, a group of five men called the Ephors, or overseers, made sure that everyone, including the kings, followed the laws. The laws were never written down, so both the memory and the judgment of the Ephors were crucial.

Herodotus, *Histories*, mid-fifth century BCE

Menander, Fragment of a play, fourth century BCE

So the Athenians found much to respect about their neighbor *polis*. But they also found much to despise. For instance, the Athenians admired eloquence. The Spartans, on the other hand, were known for being **laconic**. They thought it was a waste of time to say much. They also did not understand (or pretended not to understand) long speeches made by others, such as the Samians, another Greek people, who asked the Spartans for help. The historian Herodotus reports that

> When the people of Samos, suffering from hunger, . . . came to seek help from Sparta, they made a long speech in front of the authorities. . . . The Spartans replied that they had forgotten the first part of the request and could not understand the last. Afterwards, the Samians met with the Spartan government again, and this time they simply carried a sack and said "sack needs grain." The Spartans answered, "You did not need to say 'sack'."

Another difference was that the Athenians loved poetry and philosophy. Sparta, on the other hand, produced few poets and philosophers. So many Athenians thought they were stupid.

The way Spartan girls were raised shocked many other Greeks as well. They thought their short skirts and habit of wrestling naked were disgraceful. And the fact that some Spartan girls were taught to read and write made an Athenian writer Menander say in horror, "Teach a woman to read and write? What a thought! It's like giving extra poison to a snake that's poisonous in the first place!"

But what made the Athenians most uneasy was the great fighting strength of the Spartans. On the one hand, Athens was a powerful military force and admired the ferocity and skill of Sparta's army. On the other hand, they were worried that if this great army fought against them, Sparta might come to rule not only its own Laconia, but Attica as well.

It was only a matter of time before these two great forces had to come together to prove who was stronger. And come together they did, with results that were disastrous to both sides.

CHAPTER 13

"WOE TO THE LAND OF PERSIA!"

THE PERSIAN EMPIRE AND ITS WAR WITH GREECE

Imagine that it's a few thousands years in the future, and humans and aliens have known each other for a while and even trade goods. They look alike, but everything else about them is different: food, language, religions, customs, clothes, science, family life, government—you name it. But the humans don't trust these strange beings. What if the aliens decide to stop trading and start conquering? Many countries that normally didn't get along with each other would band together to keep the aliens out.

To many Greeks (we're back in the past now), the Persians were as alien as space beings would be to humans. Ancient people tended to be **xenophobic**, and the Greeks were no exception. They were frightened of the power of these foreigners, and didn't understand them or their culture. They were concerned that the Persians would try to take over their land and kill or enslave them. Who wouldn't want Greece? they reasoned. The Persians, they thought, would naturally crave the good life they saw the Greeks living. According to the historian Herodotus, the people in the rest of the Aegean area thought

HERODOTUS AND AESCHYLUS

*xenos + phobia =
"stranger" + "fear"
"Xenophobic" means "having
fear or hatred of foreigners."*

The Greeks were fascinated by what they saw as the "outlandish" clothing and furniture of their Persian enemies. The painter of this vase was from a Greek colony in southern Italy and chose to highlight the pointed hat and unfamiliar clothing of the Persian (center) speaking with King Darius.

Herodotus, *Histories*, mid-fifth century BCE

the Persians were only half civilized. He says that a wise man warned the king of Lydia,

> Your majesty, you are preparing to make war on people who live extremely uncomfortable lives. . . . If you conquer them, what can you get from them, since they possess nothing? But if they conquer you, think how much you will lose: once they get a taste of the good things we have, they will hold on so tightly that we will never be able to shake free of them.

The ruler of the Persian-controlled Miletus, Aristagoras, was especially worried. He tried to convince the Greek cities in Ionia that were ruled by Persia to unite against the enemy and kick them out before Persia had a chance to expand into the rest of Greece. As a reward, they, the Greeks, would then be in charge of Ionia. Aristagoras carried a bronze map with him to show the other states exactly how much territory they could take over for themselves if they got rid of the Persians.

Not everyone in the Greek world was eager to join Aristagoras. The Spartans, for example, thought that both the Persian threat and the Persian capital were too remote to be worth the trouble of going there to fight a battle that they had no guarantee of winning. And they were worried about what the *helots* might do while the soldiers were gone.

But the Athenians and some other Greeks were worried that the Persians would take over much of their trade, so they contributed some ships and sailors to the Ionian revolt. They lost. In the fighting, the Persians destroyed Aristagoras's home city of Miletus.

One of Persia's major cities, Sardis, was also leveled in this failed revolt. The Persian emperor whom the Greeks called Darius (his real name was Darayavaush) was furious at this and he attacked some Greek cities to punish them for the destruction of the city and for helping the Ionians. Darius might have attacked some Greek cities anyway, but the revolt of the Ionians gave him a good excuse.

The Greeks were terrified. The Athenians decided to send their army to Marathon to meet the threat, and they sent a

WHAT ARE YOU CALLING "SNAIL MAIL"?

Darius wasn't the first Persian ruler the Greeks knew. Darius's grandfather Cyrus had unified the Empire. He made roads and set up a postal system. The historian Herodotus wrote admiringly about these early letter carriers: "Neither rain, nor snow, nor sleet, nor hail stays these couriers from the swift completion of their appointed rounds." When the main United States post office was constructed in Washington D.C., these words were chiseled onto it.

runner to Sparta to alert the Spartans and to ask for their help. The runner supposedly covered 140 miles in one day. Although this time the Spartans saw the necessity of keeping the Persians from going any further into Greece, they decided not to leave for the battle until a religious festival was over.

So the vastly outnumbered Athenians and some other Greeks fought without Sparta at **Marathon**. Defeat looked certain, but the Greeks were better trained and had better weapons. Besides, they were fighting for their freedom, which must have given them an extra boost. They defeated the Persians. The burial mound at Marathon holds the bodies of the 192 Athenians who died. Untold thousands of Persians died in the battle.

The Greek soldiers at Marathon became great heroes. And the Athenians had proved that their army was the greatest. Most of them thought they had nothing to fear from Persia any more.

Some Greeks weren't so sure, though. The politician Themistocles was one of them.

Themistocles thought that Athens was still vulnerable and he convinced his fellow citizens to use money from their silver mines to build a great navy and to train sailors and soldiers.

This was a wise decision, because Darius had a son who was determined to do what his father had been unable to accomplish. This ruler's name was Khshararshan. There was no way most Greeks could pronounce that, so they called him Xerxes. And Xerxes was putting together a huge army and a fleet of warships to attack the Greeks.

This time Athens could not stand alone. The Persian army was just too large. Fortunately for the Greek allies, by now a wise king was ruling in Sparta. This leader was named Leonidas.

Once again, it was festival time in Greece. The ceremonies honoring the god Apollo were under way and the Olympic Games were just about to start. But Leonidas saw that Xerxes wasn't going to wait and he decided that even

{ A marathon is a long-distance foot-race of 26 miles 385 yards. This is the distance a messenger had to run to tell the Athenians of the victory at Marathon.

Pieces of ancient weaponry are still occasionally found in the field of Marathon. This sword (left) was used by a member of the infantry for hand-to-hand combat, and the arrowheads (top right) and pellets used for a slingshot (bottom right) were for fighting from a short distance.

The funeral mound of the Greek soldiers who died in the battle of Marathon still stands as a monument to their courage.

Many people think that this statue represents Leonidas, the Spartans' most revered general.

though their customs forbade them from sending a large army into battle during these holy times, it probably wouldn't hurt anything if a smaller group went. So he led 300 soldiers north. When the festivals were over, the rest of the mighty Spartan army would follow. Other Greeks joined Leonidas, and soon 10,000 soldiers arrived ready to meet the Persian force of 100,000.

Xerxes waited at a narrow pass called Thermopylae, knowing that Greek spies were reporting the size of his army back to their own people. He was convinced that the Greeks would be so terrified at the news of how many Persians were waiting for them that they would retreat. And many of them did, but not the Spartans. They spent their time exercising and combing their hair. The Persians laughed when they heard this. Little did they know that this was the way the Spartans got ready for a battle that might be their last.

Finally, Xerxes grew impatient. He ordered his men through the narrow gap, where the Greek soldiers were waiting for them. As the Persians came through, the well-disciplined Greeks slaughtered them. Xerxes ordered his troops to retreat.

The Spartans were overjoyed. They had held the Persians back from entering most of Greece, and soon the rest of their army would join them and they would chase the hated invaders from their land. All they had to do was wait for fresh troops. But a Greek traitor told Xerxes about a hidden path in the mountains that would take his soldiers around the pass and into the Greek camp, where the soldiers were resting in their tents.

Spartan sentries heard leaves rustling and saw what was happening. They ran to Leonidas to tell him that the Persians were ready to attack. A messenger from Xerxes arrived and ordered Leonidas to hand over his weapons. "Come and take them," was his defiant reply.

And Xerxes came. Leonidas was killed early in the battle. And then every single one of the Spartan soldiers, and others from different parts of Greece, died after fighting ferociously.

So Xerxes and his forces won the battle of Thermopylae. Shortly afterwards, Xerxes' army marched into Athens and burned it down (its inhabitants fled before the Persians arrived).

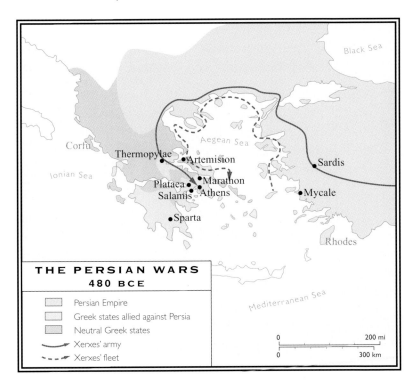

THE PERSIAN WARS

499–494 BCE
Ionian Greeks rebel against Persian king

490 BCE
Persians under Darius invade mainland Greece; Athenians defeat Persians at the Battle of Marathon

486 BCE
Darius dies and is succeeded by his son Xerxes

480 BCE
Persians defeat Spartans at Thermopylae; Greeks defeat Persians at Salamis

478 BCE
Greek *poleis* form the Delian League

But the brave Spartans had delayed the Persian advance to the south long enough for the Greek forces to gather at an island near Athens named Salamis. Themistocles tricked Xerxes into following the Greek ships into a narrow channel, where the smaller and more maneuverable Athenian ships were able to destroy the larger but clumsier Persian vessels.

The Athenian playwright Aeschylus witnessed the battle of Salamis. In his play *The Persians*, written several years later, he has a Persian messenger report,

> The Greeks behaved as if they'd caught a haul of fish,
> Stabbing the tuna with the tools at hand.
> Pieces of oar, and fragments of the wreckage
> Served them as weapons. All the sea was filled
> With screams and groans, until the dark night fell
> Upon the scene and covered it in black. . . .
> [N]ever on one day
> Have men perished like this, thousand by thousand.

Aeschylus, The Persians, 472 BCE

The Greeks were thrilled at this victory. To the Greeks, their triumph was proof that their way of life was the best and that the Persians had gotten what they deserved. Aeschylus has a Persian messenger report the defeat to his country's forces by saying in *The Persians*:

> Woe to the towns of Asia, all the towns!
> Woe to the land of Persia that once held
> Wealth beyond count! How suddenly
> Your glorious state has vanished, all at once,
> And all the honors that attend on it
> Now gone, collapsed! Woe, woe!

Persia was not actually destroyed, but the Greeks had dealt their enemy a severe blow. Athens, especially, came out ahead in this final victory. Their navy had been the crucial factor in the battle of Salamis, and when different Greek states joined together in an alliance, called the Delian League, a few years later, it was only natural to look to Athens to lead it.

AND WITH ONE HAND TIED BEHIND OUR BACKS

When a Spartan soldier was told that there were so many Persians that the sky would be thick with their arrows once the battle started, he replied coolly, "Then we'll fight in the shade."

CHAPTER 14

"THE HANDS OF THE MANY"
DEMOCRACY IN ATHENS

66 PERICLES, ISOCRATES, AND AESCHINES

Things looked rosy in the Greek *poleis* after they defeated the Persian Empire. They had emerged from the war stronger than ever, and their economies continued to grow.

Persia was still a threat, though. Maybe the next time the two forces clashed, the gods—or luck—wouldn't be on the Greek side, as they had been at Marathon and Salamis. So some of the Greek states thought it would be prudent to join together to keep an eye on things in the Aegean. With many navies patrolling the area, Persian ships would be easier to spot before they attacked anyone. And Persian vessels often carried valuable goods. To the Greeks it seemed only fair for anyone who happened upon one to loot its cargo to get revenge for the destruction that had happened on their soil.

So the *poleis* closest to Persia asked Athens to lead a new alliance. More than 100 *poleis* joined them. Modern historians call this group the Delian League because its treasury was on Delos, the island sacred to Apollo.

Not everyone thought that putting Athens in charge was such a great idea. The Spartans, for example, thought that the Athenians were getting altogether too much credit for the victories over Persia. What about Leonidas and the heroic Spartans who died at Thermopylae, after all?

At first, the Greeks were thinking of asking Sparta to head up their league. But the Spartan king acted so arrogantly that the Greeks told the Spartans to forget it and asked Athens instead. So the Spartans had to be content with leading their own alliance (which is now called the Peloponnesian League and which had already existed for several years). These two groups didn't get along at all.

A woman representing democracy crowns a man who symbolizes the Greek citizenry, showing that the people were the real rulers.

The Agora was the center of public life. The open area on the right was the marketplace, where people not only shopped but met to discuss and argue over the matters of the day. The buildings on the hill on the left housed the offices that ran the city and its religious life.

The Spartans were suspicious of the Athenian form of government, which was completely different from theirs. In Sparta, even though all citizens were supposedly equal, a small group of aristocrats made all the important decisions, from waging war and making peace to deciding which children would be exposed and which would be allowed to live. The soldiers had a vote, but they hardly ever went against what the aristocrats wanted. And the way they voted was by banging on their shields—whichever side made the most noise won.

This was quite different from the way things were run in Athens. There, the reforms of Solon had given the people some say in how they were governed. Over the years, more Athenians had achieved rights. The differences in the rights held by the various classes grew smaller and smaller until most citizens were treated very much the same. Eventually, all the important matters were decided by the people as a whole, not by the officials. This form of government is called a democracy. The Athenian statesman Pericles defined it as "the administration [of the *polis*] . . . in the hands of the many and not of the few."

Thucydides, *History of the Peloponnesian War*, 431 BCE

Some Athenians came to think that rule by the people had some problems. Many years later, the Athenian writer Isocrates, who obviously longed for the "good old days," looked back on this time and wrote in his *Antidosis* that Athens:

> grew powerful and seized the empire of the Greeks, and our fathers, growing more self-assured than was proper for them, began to look with disfavor on those good men and true who had made Athens great, envying them their power, and growing to look instead to men who were low-born and full of insolence.

So even some Athenians were skeptical about the ability of ordinary people to decide important matters.

Athens also had many government officials. The most important were:

- The ten generals (*strategoi*) in charge of the military and many civil matters as well.
- The nine *archons* in charge of political and legal matters, and with some religious duties.
- The council of 500 *bouleutai*—councilors who served a one-year term in the council preparing business for the assembly.

It's hard to be precise, but it appears there were about 100 elected officials and 600 who were chosen by lot, in addition to the 500 councilors. With so many people in charge of different functions, it was unlikely that anyone would take over the whole government.

This was no accident. The Athenians set things up this way because they were worried about any one person or group of people getting too much power. They had not forgotten the tyrants and they had no intention of ever again being ruled by someone with such power. In fact, they were so afraid of a single ruler that some people thought that their most popular leader, Pericles, always wore his helmet because someone had told him that without it he resembled the tyrant Peisistratus.

So, to keep one power-hungry man from gaining too much control, an *archon* couldn't serve more than one year.

> 66 Isocrates, *Antidosis*, 354 BCE

ANCIENT LITTERBUGS

You might call clay jars the "plastic bags of the ancient world." They were used for carrying and storing all sorts of things. You could reach down to the ground in any town in the Mediterranean and be reasonably sure of touching a part of a broken pot. Archaeologists use them to get dates and other information about archaeological sites. If you find a Greek pot in Italy, for example, you know that the Greeks were trading or living in that part of Europe.

THEMISTOCLES AND ARISTIDES

Aristides was an Athenian *archon* and general. Soon after the Battle of Marathon, a huge amount of silver was found near Athens. Aristides wanted to divide it evenly among all the citizens, but his rival Themistocles had a different idea. He wanted to use it to build ships for the Athenian navy. They couldn't agree or compromise, and finally the Athenians voted to exile him for ten years, so off he went.

When Xerxes attacked a few years later, Themistocles asked his fellow-citizens to allow Aristides to come back early. They agreed, which was a good thing for Athens—Aristides played an important role in the defeat of the Persians.

And to keep any person from persuading everyone to vote for him, the *archons* were chosen by a kind of lottery. The Athenians figured that it wasn't really important to choose the most capable person to do an *archon's* job, so choosing by lot was just fine. If an *archon* made a bad decision, it could always be changed. And most decisions were made by the people, voting in the assembly.

But if a general made a mistake, the consequences could be disastrous. What if Themistocles had decided to fight the Persians at some other place than Salamis? The Greeks might have lost. The very idea was terrifying. So generals were elected to increase the chances of having only competent people in the post. Generals also had a great deal of input into how the government was run during times of peace, too, and they were allowed to hold office as many times as they could get elected. Pericles served as general more than thirty times.

When any matter came up for a vote, the *ekklesia*, or assembly, met. All eligible citizens could come to the meetings and voice their opinions, and most important, they could all vote. The *strategoi* presented their ideas first and then anyone who wanted to add an opinion could speak. And they didn't just speak—they yelled, laughed, applauded, booed, cheered. It must have been very noisy and chaotic, especially since thousands of people might show up at a meeting. Athens had a direct democracy: all the eligible people voted on everything. *All* of them.

The orator Aeschines was enthusiastic about the way anyone who wanted to express himself was allowed, and even encouraged, to do so. He said in a speech that class and wealth distinctions make no difference and that the official running the assembly

66 Aeschines, *Against Timorchus,* 345 BCE

does not exclude from the platform the man whose ancestors have not held a general's office, nor even the man who earns his daily bread by working at a trade; nay, these men he most heartily welcomes and for this reason he repeats again, and again the invitation, "Who wishes to address the assembly?"

Some—actually, most—people were not allowed to participate. These included women, children, slaves, foreigners, men who had shown cowardice in war, and those who had wasted their inheritance. Athenians who were traveling or lived too far away couldn't make their voices heard either.

If a citizen had done something really bad—or if his political enemies just wanted to get rid of him—there was always ostracism. Ostracism meant sending someone into exile for ten years. Its name derives from the word for "broken pot": *ostrakon*. In those days, paper was extremely expensive, but pieces of pottery were easy to come by. If an Athenian wanted to get rid of someone, he didn't even have to accuse his enemy of a crime. All he had to do was to wait for the next ostracism. Each April, the citizens were asked if they wanted to hold an ostracism that year. If the majority voted in favor, another meeting would be held, and everyone present would be given an *ostrakon*. On it he could write down the name of anyone he thought was a danger to the state. If enough pieces had the same name on it, that person would be kicked out of Athens. After ten years, he could return home and pick up his life where he had left off.

Democracy may not seem like that big a deal to many people today who have lived in democracies all their lives. It sometimes seems that every time the TV is on, someone's talking about an election in some part of the world. Even people with other forms of government have heard of the democratic system.

But for the people of the ancient world, this was a brand-new, exciting, and sometimes scary idea. Let regular, ordinary people decide things? How can you trust them? What if they choose the wrong way? Why not find one strong, smart man or at least a group of aristocrats and turn all the decisions over to them, as in most other *poleis*? No wonder most of the world rejected the idea of democracy for a long, long time. Many countries still do.

Pericles summed up a great deal of what it meant to be a citizen in a funeral oration, given after many of Athens' citizens were killed in the Peloponnesian War. Some of his statements include:

STUFFING THE BALLOT BOX

Most Athenians couldn't write, or it at least found it difficult. So the person who called for the ostracism would hire someone to write the name of his political enemy on many *ostraka*. Archaeologists have found a bunch of nearly 200 *ostraka* in a well on the Acropolis with the name "Themistocles" written on them in only a few different handwritings.
Someone must have hung around outside the meeting, passing these out to the people on their way in to vote!

Thucydides, *The History of the Peloponnesian War*, 431 BCE

Our government does not copy that of our neighbors. Rather, we serve as an example to them.

In our public life we are not exclusive, and in our private business we are not suspicious of one another. We do not get angry with our neighbor for doing what he likes or give him nasty looks which, though they would not cause physical harm, are still painful.

Even without the kind of laborious training they have in Sparta, we meet danger with peace of mind, and our courage is gained by habit, not enforced by law.

It is right that we consider those who have the clearest knowledge of pleasure and pain but do not shrink from danger because of it as the bravest men of all.

But there were certainly some problems with the Athenian system. First of all, most people in Athens couldn't participate. Also, there was a lot of bribery around election time. This meant that wealthier people, who could afford to buy votes, got what they wanted more often than was fair. And sometimes people would get carried away with the emotions of the moment and make decisions based on what everyone was saying, rather than on what they really believed would be best.

But as Britain's prime minister, Winston Churchill, said in 1947, "democracy is the worst form of Government except for all those other forms that have been tried from time to time."

Some people said that Pericles wore a helmet to hide his receding hairline. Others claimed that he was bothered by a resemblance to the unpopular tyrant Peisistratus and wore a helmet so they would look less like each other. This is a marble copy, made by a Roman artist, of a bronze statue that was destroyed long ago.

CHAPTER 15

HOPLITES AND TRIREMES
WARFARE

“ TYRTAEUS,
HOMER, PLUTARCH,
XENOPHON, AND
EURIPIDES

Here is courage, mankind's finest possession, here is
    the noblest prize that a young man can endeavor
    to win,
And it is a good thing his polis and all the people
    share with him
When a man plants his feet and stands in the fore-
    most spears
Relentlessly, all thought of foul flight completely
    forgotten,
And has trained his heart to be steadfast and to
    endure,
And with words encourages the man who is stationed
    beside him.

“ Tyrateus, untitled poem,
late seventh century BCE

The poet Tyrtaeus was expressing the feelings of many Greeks when he composed these verses. It seems that the Greeks admired soldiers and thought bravery was the highest virtue.

Someone once said that ancient Greece was a place where once in a while peace broke out. Of course, this is an exaggeration. Still, when they weren't actually fighting, the Greeks were usually preparing for war, recovering from war, or keeping an eye on their neighbors in case they were getting ready to attack.

So even in the rare times of peace, war was never far from anyone's mind. The Spartans, for example, had built their whole society around preparing for conflict. Reminders of war were everywhere in Sparta.

Athenian culture wasn't as organized around the military, but the Athenians knew that their city's patron deity, Athena, was also the goddess of war. Any time an Athenian went into her temple, the Parthenon, the towering statue of the goddess in full armor loomed over the visitor. In her huge hand she held the figure of the goddess Nike, or victory.

Even Greek sports were a kind of preparation for war. The most important events in the Olympics were wrestling, racing, and other events that conditioned men for battle and tested their courage and physical skills.

War was so important that one deity wasn't enough to take care of it, so the god Ares presided over battle. Athena had many other functions, but all Ares cared about was fighting. It didn't matter to him who was right or wrong, as long as blood was shed. In the *Iliad,* a long poem mostly about war, the poet Homer has Ares's father, Zeus, calling him "most hateful of all the gods who hold Olympus. Forever quarreling is dear to your heart, war and battles."

Athena was ferocious, too. But she didn't seem to enjoy fighting, seeing it as a necessary means to an end rather than as fun, like Ares.

So what were the Greeks always fighting about?

There are many causes of war. Sometimes a nation will claim that it is trying to bring justice or a better form of government to an oppressed nation. Two other important reasons are conquest and economics. There's not really much difference between the two, since power and wealth go together. Strictly economic reasons for war would include gaining control over trade routes, controlling an area that has assets that you want, and plundering the conquered area for goods.

Since the threat of war was constant, most Greek cities were well fortified. Even back in Mycenaean times, towns had huge defensive walls to protect the inhabitants from raids. Settlements were frequently built on hills, which could be more easily defended, and high walls protected them. Sparta was an exception. Their city was in the middle of a plain and the Spartans scorned putting up defensive walls. They were daring anyone to attack.

❝ Homer, *Iliad*, about 750 BCE

The god of war Ares (left) battles a giant, while another giant lies dead on the ground. In works of art, Ares is usually shown with helmet, shield, and spear.

Greece is a land of rough mountains, beaches, plains, and sea. Armed forces had to be prepared to fight in many kinds of terrain and against enemies with many kinds of weapons. Since so much of Greece is coastline, and boats are an efficient way to get around, attack by sea was common from the earliest days.

A major improvement in naval warfare came in the sixth century BCE, with a boat called the trireme. It was quickly and easily built. It was light, which made it easily maneuverable, but also fragile. A trireme had sails, but no rudder, so the sails could be used only if the wind was blowing in the direction that the boat needed to go. The major source of power was the oarsmen. A trireme could cover over 200 miles without stopping, at a speed of about 9 miles per hour. This might not sound like much, but it was breathtaking in those days.

Fighting on land was also crucial. Early in the history of Greek warfare, men riding on horseback and in chariots were a major force in land battles. Since both horses and chariots were terribly expensive, only the wealthiest men could afford them. Most soldiers marched and fought on foot. The usual method of fighting was for the two opposing armies to stand far apart and throw spears at each other.

Greek ships were amazingly fast and easy to handle. They were sometimes powered by both wind and muscle, as is this modern replica. The three rows of oars identify this boat as a trireme. If it had two rows, it would be a bireme. It took a great deal of skill and practice for the oarsmen to row swiftly without getting their oars tangled.

But as the *poleis* and democracy grew, so did the idea of more people defending their homeland. Starting in the seventh century BCE, a new kind of soldier became the backbone of most Greek armies: the heavily armed *hoplite* (from *hoplon*, the word for "shield"). Hoplites were *really* heavily armed— the helmet, breastplate, greaves (shin guards), sword, and shield weighed between 50 and 70 pounds. This would be a burden today and must have seemed even heavier then, when people were generally smaller than they are now.

These weapons were made of expensive metal, but still, they cost less than a horse and its equipment, not to mention a chariot. This meant that more men could fight for their *polis*. As middle-class men contributed more to the military, they started demanding more rights in politics. So the changes in the army and the growth of democracy grew hand in hand.

Hoplites moved in an organized unit called a phalanx, rows of soldiers usually 8 to 12 men deep. The main **tactic** was for two opposing armies to advance slowly upon each other and, when they were about one hundred yards apart, to break into a run and start fighting. Both sides would be yelling a war cry as they went.

Ancient war must have been deafening—the rattling armor, the whinnying horses, the shouting men. Homer says in the *Iliad* that when the Greeks and Trojans met,

> Not such is the roaring against dry land of the sea's surf
> As it rolls in from the open under the hard blast of
> the north wind;

"Tactic" comes from *taktike*, which means "the art of arrangement." It now means a plan, especially of battle.

📖 Homer, *Iliad*, about 750 BCE

Chariot horses had to be strong and swift, and highly trained not to run away from the terrifying noise and chaos of battle.

Bronze armor was very expensive and only the wealthiest soldiers could afford a complete set, like this Sicilian one. The curved implement on the right is a strigil, used to scrape dirt and sweat off the skin.

Not such is the bellowing of fire in its blazing
In the deep places of the hills when it rises inflaming
 the forest,
Nor such again the crying voice of the wind in the
 deep-haired
Oaks, when it roars highest in its fury against them,
Not so loud as now the noise of Achaians [Greeks]
 and Trojans
In voice of terror rose as they drove against one
 another.

Phalanx war differed from the earlier form of combat, like the Trojan War described by Homer, where soldiers threw spears from a long distance. Now the warriors on the same side stood close together with their shields overlapping to make a solid wall. The two sides would be pressed against each other and fighting was face-to-face. It was noisy, chaotic, terrifying, and bloody. In at least one case the generals put friends and relatives near each other so that soldiers would be motivated to fight to save not only their own lives, but the lives of people they loved. In his *Life of Pelopidas* the biographer and essayist Plutarch notes that

a band of men united by ties of love is truly indissoluble and unbreakable, for each man . . . fears the disgrace

66 Plutarch, *Life of Pelopidas,* about 100 CE

Weapons were for show as well as for fighting. This dagger-sheath with very expensive decoration demonstrates its owner's wealth.

that would come from failing in the face of the other, and each will stand his ground in the face of danger in order to protect the other.

The aftermath of the battle wasn't much better. The historian Xenophon describes it like this in his *Life of Agesilaus:*

> 66 Xenophon, *Life of Agesilaus,* early fourth century BCE

Now that the fighting was at an end, a weird spectacle met the eye, as one surveyed the scene of the conflict— the earth stained with blood, friend and foe lying dead side by side, shields smashed to pieces, spears snapped in two, daggers bared of their sheaths, some on the ground, some embedded in the bodies, some yet gripped by the hand.

Survivors on the losing side were executed, or held for ransom, or taken into slavery, which was often a death sentence.

Civilians didn't fare any better. Soldiers often burned houses, fields, and property in order to weaken their enemy even further. If their homes were destroyed, people not taken as slaves or killed outright might starve to death or die from exposure.

So warfare was brutal and ugly. Both soldiers and civilians died painful deaths. Towns were destroyed, farmlands were made useless, and families were torn apart. The playwright Euripides showed the pain felt by both the victor and the vanquished in his play *The Trojan Women,* about the aftermath of the Trojan War. A Greek messenger reluctantly has to tell the wife of the Trojan prince Hector the harsh fate that her young son is to suffer:

A MONUMENT TO ARMS

After a battle, the victorious side would construct a monument made of arms and other objects they had taken from their defeated enemy. They called it a *trophaion,* from a word meaning "defeat." The word "trophy" derives from *trophaion.*

> 66 Euripides, *The Trojan Women,* 415 BCE

He must be thrown from the high walls of Troy.
If you are wise, you will not cling to him.
No, bear your sorrows with a noble heart.
Do not imagine you have power when you don't. . . .
If you do anything to make the army angry,
This boy will lie unburied on the ground.

CHAPTER 16

THE GREEK WORLD WAR
THE PELOPONNESIAN WAR

This was the situation after the Greek victory in the Persian Wars: Athens was the head of the newly-formed Delian League, which included many islands and city-states that felt uncomfortable with the Persian Empire looming over them. The Delian League had a good army and a great navy. Athens was connected to its port city Piraeus by the Long Walls, a fortification that meant the city always had access to the sea. Trade would go on uninterrupted even if Athens was under attack, so it would be impossible to starve the Athenians into submission.

Meanwhile, Sparta was the head of the older Peloponnesian League, which included the *polis* of Corinth. Corinth had a powerful navy and competed with Athens for trade. Sparta's infantry was strong and well disciplined. The Spartan soldiers wore matching uniforms (unusual for

**SPARTAN AND ATHENIAN
ALLIES IN THE
PELOPONNESIAN WAR**

Athenian league   Spartan allies

Even in ruins, the temple of Apollo at Corinth still dominates the area. The city's strategic location made it an important ally for Sparta.

Plutarch, *Life of Lycurgus*, about 100 CE

that time) and drilled together. Their unity was intimidating, as the biographer Plutarch says in his biography of the Spartan law-giver Lycurgus:

> It was terrifying but also magnificent to see them when they marched in step with the rhythms of their flutes, with no gap in their line of battle, and no disorder in their minds, but with calm expressions on their faces moving with the music to the deadly fight.

Athens and Sparta had never really gotten along, so even though they had joined together against Persia, they were keeping an eye on each other. They had occasional fights, so to keep things calm, in 445 BCE the two *poleis* signed a temporary treaty called the Thirty Years' Peace. They figured that after the 30 years were up, they could review the terms and sign again if they wanted.

But the peace collapsed long before the 30 years were up. Trouble broke out between Corinth and its colony Corcyra, which didn't belong to either league. The Corcyraeans had the second-largest navy in Greece (after Athens) and asked Athens to support them. They warned Athens that if Corinth conquered Corcyra in a war, the Corinthians would then have a huge navy to use to help Sparta if the Spartan and Athenian leagues ever had a war. Pericles agreed, saying that he saw a "cloud of war over the Peloponnesus." Soon,

Athenian sailors were fighting against Corinth—a member of the Peloponnesian League. It's not surprising that Sparta didn't like this at all.

Then Athens forbade a Spartan ally to trade in any ports belonging to the Delian League (which controlled almost all the ports). There wasn't much reason for this prohibition aside from annoying Sparta. The Spartans asked the Athenians to change their minds, but they refused.

The Spartans were led by a wise king. He and Pericles were friends, so he knew how powerful the Athenians were. He warned his people that they weren't ready to fight, since they were low on money and ships. He told them that their children would still be fighting this war after they themselves died. This was a serious warning, since most Greek wars were quite short-lived.

But the Spartans were angry at how the Athenians were treating their allies and fearful of the way Athens kept expanding its power. So they voted for war and the Spartan king was forced to lead an army into Athenian territory.

Pericles came up with a plan: everyone should come inside the city walls where they would live off food and supplies brought into the Athenian harbor town Piraeus by boat. Meanwhile, the Spartans would wander around looking for someone to fight and would eventually give up and go home.

This plan might have worked except for two problems. First, the Athenians didn't like the idea of hiding from the enemy. They knew that everyone would say that they were scared that the Spartan army was better than theirs (and they were probably right).

But there was soon a bigger problem, and one that wasn't caused by people—not directly, at least. A plague hit Athens and with everyone living so close together, it spread rapidly. No known disease fits all the symptoms described by Thucydides: raging thirst, rash, red eyes, a swollen mouth, cough, vomiting, irritated skin, diarrhea. Death usually followed within a week. Few survived and those who did sometimes lost their fingers and toes and even their memory.

It raged for four years, during which between one-quarter and one-third of the inhabitants of the city (including

What Was Plaguing the Athenians?

"Plague" comes from the word *plege*, which means "a blow or wound." A plague is a disease that infects a lot of people and kills many of them. Thucydides, who lived through the plague described it in his *History of the Peloponnesian War*:

"*No pestilence of such extent or mortality was remembered in any part of the world. Physicians were no match for it, and they died in the largest numbers, since it was they who visited the sick most often. . . . Prayers in the temples and things like that turned out to be so pointless that finally the overwhelming nature of the disaster led people to abandon them altogether*"

"They love, they hate, they cannot do without him." The Athenian playwright Aristophanes captured his countrymen's feelings toward the complicated personality of Alcibiades (above) in these words.

As armies became more professional, it became more important for the *strategos* (the military-political leader) to use clever strategies as well as strength to win battles.

Pericles) died. Sick and discouraged, the Athenians gave up on staying inside the city and marched out to battle the Spartans.

They fought for years. The Spartans tried to keep the combat on land and the Athenians used their navy to attack Spartan allies near the sea. Each side won sometimes and lost sometimes. At one point a group of Spartans who were stuck on an island surrendered to the Athenians. The other Greeks were shocked that the usually valiant Spartans would lay down their arms. In 421 BCE, Athens and Sparta signed a new truce. But it didn't last long.

Pericles had raised an orphaned nephew named Alcibiades. This young man seems to have shared his uncle's charisma and intelligence, but not much of his loyalty or emotional stability. He had inherited an enormous fortune from his father and was very handsome. But he was also eccentric. He once cut off the tail of his own beautiful and expensive dog. When he was asked why, he said that he knew people were going to talk about all the strange things he did and if he did this one *really* strange thing, they would gossip less about the rest.

Alcibiades was a brave soldier and risked his life in battle to save Socrates, the philosopher who was also his teacher and friend. But this wasn't enough. What he wanted more than anything else was to be famous. It must have been hard for an ambitious person to grow up in the house of someone as well known and important as Pericles. It would be difficult to do something so amazing that people would stop referring to him as "Pericles's ward" and admire him for his own accomplishments.

He decided to enter politics and in 420 BCE was elected *strategos*. He convinced the Athenians to let him attack Sicily. A more experienced *strategos* was to go along.

But before they set sail, some unknown person or persons vandalized the sacred statues of Hermes, which were supposed to protect the city. People suspected Alcibiades and his rowdy friends of committing this sacrilege. Worse, they thought that the angered gods would frown on their expedition and it would fail.

Alcibiades left for Sicily anyway. While he was away, his political enemies continued accusing him of this crime and added that he and his friends had also made fun of rituals worshiping the harvest goddess Demeter. Athenian authorities sent messengers to Sicily to tell Alcibiades to come back to be tried. Saying that it would be stupid to risk a trial when he could just escape, Alcibiades went over to the Spartan side.

Both sides continued to pour troops into Sicily, but the conflict ended in disaster for the Athenians. They were defeated in a naval battle with a great loss of life. Many of the survivors were dragged off to brutal conditions as slaves in the Sicilian city of Syracuse.

The Spartans got just as tired of Alcibiades's antics as the Athenians had been. For one thing, Alcibiades had a romance with the wife of a Spartan king. Worse, he was forming a friendship with Persia. Alcibiades suggested that the Persians (who were helping the Spartans) should stand back while the two enemies fought it out among themselves. Eventually, he reasoned, both sides would grow so weak that Persia could step in and take over.

When Persia stopped helping Sparta, Athens thought that Alcibiades was working on their side and invited him back. He accepted and was elected *strategos* again. He won several important victories for Athens and was admired even by his vanquished enemies, since he treated them with mercy.

But then the Athenians blamed Alcibiades for a defeat and removed him from command. He still had some feelings for his homeland, however. He was sitting in his villa when he saw that the Athenian and

These two soldiers were killed in the Peloponnesian War. They must have been good friends to be pictured together on their funeral monument.

INSTANT MESSENGER, GREEK-STYLE

The first written messages to be transmitted through the air were notes attached to arrows that Greeks shot to each other during a battle in northern Greece.

Spartan fleets were about to have a battle in the bay right underneath his house. He rode down to tell the Athenian leader that the Athenians were in a dangerous place and gave them advice on how to handle themselves better. But they ignored him.

The result was a catastrophe. Plutarch reports in his biography of Alcibiades:

Plutarch, *Life of Alcibiades*, about 100 CE

> Events soon proved that Alcibiades was right about the situation, for the Spartan admiral fell upon them suddenly, when they weren't expecting it at all. Only the *strategos* Conon escaped, with eight triremes. The rest of the ships, almost two hundred, were captured and taken away, along with their crews, which amounted to three thousand men. These sailors were executed.

Xenophon says in his history *The Hellenica* that when word of this defeat reached the port city,

Xenophon, *The Hellenica*, early fourth century BCE

> the sound of wailing passed from Piraeus through the long walls to the city, each person passing the news on to the next. That night no one slept. Rather, they were occupied in grieving not only for those who had already died but also, in fact much more so, for themselves, believing that they would suffer the same treatment they had dealt out to others.

And they had good reason to mourn. Shortly after the battle, the Spartans captured Athens and tore down the city walls. They set up a new government, with a group of pro-Spartan oligarchs ruling the once-proud leader of the Delian League. Except for a brief alliance in the fourth century BCE, it would be more than 2,000 years before Athens once again became a political leader. In the 19th century, when the Hellenic Republic (which most of us simply call the country of Greece) was formed, Athens was chosen as its capital.

Today, newspapers carry lists of people killed in wars. When this inscription of Athenian casualties from the Peloponnesian War was made, a more permanent record was left in stone. Modern historians use documents like this to double-check ancient accounts of battles.

CHAPTER 17

TAKE TWO VULTURE'S EGGS AND CALL ME IN THE MORNING

SCIENCE AND MEDICINE

The ancient Greeks divided their studies into subjects, just like today, but their dividing lines were usually very different from what they are today. For example, ancient Greeks learned history from the works of the poet Homer. Nowadays, we view Homer's *Iliad* and *Odyssey* as literature. And while today we put physics, biology, and chemistry in the category of science, the ancient Greeks saw the sciences as a kind of philosophy.

This makes sense if you realize that ancient people didn't rely on scientific experimentation to find out how things work. Instead, they investigated the world around them by observing (looking and drawing conclusions based on what you see) and speculating (wondering and taking educated guesses). This is pretty much how philosophers work, too. They observe, think, make guesses, and discuss their ideas with others.

Scientists and mathematicians were the first Greeks to move away from relying on myths to explain the world and toward systematic observation. Greek scientists had the benefit of the great thinkers who had come before them, especially in Egypt and in Mesopotamia. The Greeks certainly came up with many new and often revolutionary ideas, but they didn't have to start from scratch. With the help of the thinkers who had come before them, they discovered and invented some amazing things. The fact that their number system didn't have a zero makes their mathematical achievements even more impressive.

Here are some of these thinkers:

Pythagoras was from Ionia and lived in the sixth century BCE. He thought that numbers could explain the universe.

Popular ancient Greek writers were lucky—their works were copied over so many times that much of what they wrote has survived the centuries. But in some cases, all that is known about some less influential thinkers comes from scraps like this papyrus found in 1892, which discusses medicine.

He was one of the first people to see the relationship between numbers and music, for example. He thought that *harmonia* ("fitting together") was what made the orderly world arise out of the chaos that existed at the beginning of time, and that numbers were the way this fitting together happened. Numbers even stood for ideas. The idea of justice, for example, was represented by the number four. Marriage was five. (People are still trying to figure out exactly what this means.)

Pythagoras's best-known mathematical idea is called the Pythagorean theorem. It tells how to figure out how long one side of a right triangle is if you know the length of the other two sides.

Pythagoras was also a philosopher who thought that when someone dies, his or her soul gets reborn in an animal. The Pythagoreans were strict vegetarians because they didn't want to risk eating an animal with a person's soul. A story tells that Pythagoras once said to a man beating a dog, "Stop! Stop now! The spirit of that dog was once my friend. I recognized his voice when the dog yelped."

Many of the followers of Pythagoras were women. His

Pythagoras said that "animals have intelligence and emotions, but only humans have reason."

wife, Theano, ran his school after his death. She wrote many treatises, including *The Golden Mean,* which discussed balance and harmony and which has been influential in Western thought, especially art, ever since.

Democritus was born in the fifth century BCE. Some of his ideas turned out to be amazingly accurate. He said that most of the universe is a big nothingness and little particles float around in it. Many ancient people thought this was ridiculous. If this were true, the skeptics said, then nothing could move, since motion means going from one thing to another. If there isn't something to move to, you aren't really moving.

Democritus also said that if you keep cutting things into smaller and smaller pieces, you will eventually have a tiny piece, the **atomon**, that can't be divided any further. Democritus thought that colors come about from the different ways *atoma* (the plural of *atomon*) are arranged in an object. Strange as this idea may seem, it turns out that he was right.

> *a + tom* = "not" + "to cut" Scientists used to think that the atom was the smallest particle of matter and could not be divided. You can see *tom* in many medical words: In a tonsillectomy, tonsils are cut out. What's cut out if you have an appendectomy?

According to Democritus, belief in the gods came about when people couldn't come up with rational explanations for natural occurrences, so they assumed that some supernatural being had to be at work making thunder, causing plagues, and bringing about other phenomena they couldn't explain.

Archimedes was born in Syracuse (in Sicily, now part of Italy) in about 290 BCE. He used arithmetic to study many aspects of the world, including the movements of the planets.

His most famous achievement was figuring out if a craftsman had cheated the king. The king had given the craftsman some gold to make a crown. The finished crown weighed the same amount as the piece of gold, but the king was suspicious that the craftsman had kept some of the gold for himself and had mixed some other less expensive metal in with it.

Since metals have different weights, the craftsman would have had to use either a larger or a smaller piece of the replacement metal to keep the crown the same weight as the original piece of gold. So the crown would be larger or smaller than the king's piece of gold if there were some other kind of metal mixed in.

The problem was that the crown had points and balls and irregular shapes, so it couldn't be measured accurately.

Supposedly, Archimedes was thinking about this problem when he decided to take a bath. The bathtub was filled to the brim, and when he stepped into it, it overflowed. It occurred to him that the amount of water that spilled out was the same size as the part of his body that he put into it: If he put in a toe, only a few drops would overflow, but if he put in his whole leg, more would come out.

So if he filled a bowl with water and put into it a lump of gold the same size as the one the king had given the craftsman, he could catch the water that spilled out and measure it. Then he could fill the bowl again, put the crown in, and see if the same amount of overflow was produced. If the crown was larger or smaller than the lump of gold, the amount of water that came out would be greater or lesser.

The legend says that Archimedes was so excited to have thought of this that he ran naked through the streets of Syracuse, shouting "Eureka!," which means "I've found it!" (It turns out that the goldsmith had indeed cheated the king.)

Archimedes got so caught up in his work that supposedly he was killed because he wouldn't leave it. The biographer Plutarch reports in the *Life of Marcellus* that

Plutarch, *Life of Marcellus*, about 100 CE

Archimedes was wrapped up in working out some problem that involved a diagram. With both his mind and his eyes fixed on the subject of the speculation, he never noticed that the Romans had burst into the city and captured it . . . and so when a Roman soldier surprised him by coming up to him and ordering him to follow him to his commander Marcellus, he refused, because he wasn't completely finished with the problem on which he was working. Enraged, the soldier drew his sword and ran him through.

Eratosthenes was also from a part of the Greek world that now isn't Greek: Cyrene, in what is now Libya. He settled in the Greek city of Alexandria, Egypt, in about 255 BCE.

Many people today think that nobody wanted to give Christopher Columbus money to sail west to the Indies

An angry Roman soldier killed Archimedes when he refused to leave his work and follow the soldier's orders. The soldier was later executed for his crime.

because in 1490s everybody believed that the world was flat. But this isn't true. The Greeks (almost 2,000 years earlier) had already figured out that the world was a sphere, and in fact Eratosthenes figured out the earth's size.

Hippocrates of Cos is best known for the Hippocratic Oath, a pledge that many new doctors still take in which they swear to behave honorably.

> I swear by Apollo the physician, and Aesculapius, and Health, and All-heal, and all the gods and goddesses, that, according to my ability and judgment, I will keep this Oath. . . . I will follow that system of regimen which, according to my ability and judgment, I consider for the benefit of my patients, and abstain from whatever is deleterious and mischievous. . . . Whatever, in connection with my professional practice or not, in connection with it, I see or hear, in the life of men, which ought not to be spoken of abroad, I will not divulge, as reckoning that all such should be kept secret. While I continue to keep this Oath

Hippocrates, *The Oath,* 400 BCE

CENTERS OF SCIENTIFIC AND MEDICAL EXPLORATION IN THE GREEK WORLD

unviolated, may it be granted to me to enjoy life and the practice of the art, respected by all men, in all times! But should I trespass and violate this Oath, may the reverse be my lot!

This oath is very similar to a much older one from Egypt. Little is known about Hippocrates's life other than that he lived in the fifth century BCE.

Hippocrates's main contribution to medical science was his insistence that there is a reason behind illnesses. He said that doctors were embarrassed to admit that they couldn't figure out the cause of **epilepsy** and other conditions and so blamed it on the gods. The only sacred part of illness, Hippocrates said, was the holy bond between the doctor and his patients.

Hypatia also came from an area outside of what is now Greece: Egypt. She was born about 370 CE, so she lived much later than most of the other well-known Greek scientists. She lectured in mathematics and philosophy in the city of Alexandria. Unfortunately for Hypatia, the times in which she lived were very dangerous for people who praised non-Christian ideas, and she was murdered.

"Epilepsy" comes from *epilepsia*, which means "a taking hold." This disease can cause people to lose consciousness and have muscle spasms. People with epilepsy cannot control their movements during a seizure and it may look like some supernatural force has grabbed them.

It took a long time for some of the ideas of these scientists to be accepted by the general public. Often, people prefer to believe what they've always been told and refuse to accept new theories. Some Greek scientists had a hard time convincing those around them that they were right.

For instance, a scientist named Aglaonike could predict eclipses of the moon. You'd think that after she was proven right, people would believe her. But instead, she was regarded as a sorceress. Apparently some people couldn't tell the difference between predicting an event and causing it.

And although most educated Greeks believed Eratosthenes and the other scientists who said that the world was a sphere, almost everyone else believed what their eyes told them: that the earth is flat.

Greek scientists believed things that nowadays look pretty odd. Some of it isn't their fault—they didn't have telescopes and microscopes and precise measuring instruments. Also, nobody had yet come up with the idea of carefully controlled scientific experiments. If something made sense, they figured it was probably true.

So if they thought that the earth stood still and the rest of the universe revolved around it, that's understandable. It took almost 2,000 years before astronomers understood the real situation. If they thought that a bad line-up of the stars caused diseases, they can't be blamed for not knowing about the existence of microbes. Who could believe that something so tiny that you can't even see could kill a human?

But even if they got some of the facts wrong, the ancient Greeks managed to push Western science into the direction it has followed ever since. Observation, seeking a rational explanation for events, and willingness to explore new ideas are still the most important parts of scientific exploration.

THE HEAD BONE'S CONNECTED TO WHAT?

The Greeks learned a lot from the Egyptians in the field of anatomy. When the Egyptians mummified their dead, they usually removed many of the body's internal organs. That way, they found out a great deal about how the human body was put together.

Hypatia was a teacher of philosophy as well as a mathematician and astronomer.

CHAPTER 18

"FREED FROM THE CLASH OF ARMS"
THE OLYMPIC GAMES

66 Bacchylides, *Ode*, early fifth century BCE

Strum
And craft for us . . . well-woven songs
For Argeius, the junior boxer,
Victor at the Isthmian games.

When the poet Bacchylides wrote this poem asking the Muses to sing about an athlete, he was putting into words what many of his fellow Greeks felt about sports. For the Greeks, the games held at Olympia, Nemea, and other sites were among the most important parts of their lives.

People use different events from their history as the starting point when they count years. The Year One of the Muslim calendar (corresponding to 622 CE), for instance, is set by the journey of the Prophet Mohammed to Medina. The Jewish calendar starts at what some Jews believe to be the creation of the world in 3761 BCE. The ancient Romans counted from the founding of their city, which they thought had taken place in 753 BCE. For a time, France used a calendar that began with the French Revolution in the 18th century.

The establishment of a religion, the creation of the world, a new civilization, a revolution—these are all such important events that it's easy to see why a society would think of them as a turning point in its history. So what important, earth-shattering, crucial event did the ancient Greeks choose as *their* start?

The crouching stance of a discus thrower was ideal for the artist who painted this plate, as it made it easier to fit a human form into the circular shape.

They chose the first Olympic Games, in 776 BCE.

Games? Why were games, of all things, so important?

The Greek *poleis* were highly competitive with each other. They had very different ways of life: different governments, customs, favorite gods, and ways of worshiping them. But at Olympia, where games were held to honor Zeus, they could rediscover and celebrate what they had in common. Only Greeks could participate in the ancient Olympics and only men could compete. So the Games were a celebration of the strong, healthy Greek male.

Also, although different gods were important in different city-states, most Greeks believed in the same group of gods and acknowledged that Zeus was their king and leader. So by worshiping Zeus at the Games in his holy city of Olympia, the contestants and spectators were honoring all the gods together.

But that's where the togetherness ended. The athletes fought hard to beat each other. There were no second- or third-place medals. Either you won or you lost, and these fierce competitors hated to lose. The Spartans wouldn't even participate in some events for fear of being disgraced by defeat.

Most of the events were track and field, with a sprint called the *stadion* being one of the most important. Only the

NO WOMEN ALLOWED

Some historians think that single women were allowed to watch the Olympic Games. There was a rumor that a married woman caught sneaking a peek at men in competition was thrown off a cliff head-first, but some Greeks doubted this. After a while, women were allowed one race, the Heraea, in honor of the goddess Hera.

The competitors ran through this entry to the stadium at Olympia to be greeted by the cheers of thousands of spectators.

OLYMPIA

best athletes attempted the pentathlon, which combined the *stadion*, the long jump, the javelin throw, the discus throw, and wrestling. And you had to be not only skilled but brave to participate in the *pankration*, a combination of wrestling and boxing where just about the only rules were that you couldn't bite your opponent or attempt to gouge out his eyes with your thumbs (fingers were allowed). The athlete would wrap his fists in hard oxhide so that when he hit his opponent, he would really injure him.

Some writers admired the athletes so much that they made claims for them that couldn't possibly be true. Athenaeus, who wrote about food and eating, says admiringly in *The Gastronomers* that an athlete named Milo of Kroton

❝ Athenaeus, *The Gastronomers*, about 200 CE

used to eat twenty pounds of meat and twenty of bread and wash it down with eight quarts of wine. At Olympia he lifted a four-year-old bull onto his shoulders and carried it around the stadium, and then butchered it and ate it in one day with no help from anyone.

A pankratist named Polydamas was constantly trying to prove that he was as tough as the hero Herakles, and according to what the travel writer Pausanias says in his *Description of Greece,* to test his strength he once

❝ Pausanias, *Description of Greece*, second century CE

went into a herd of cattle and grabbed the biggest, fiercest bull by one of its hind legs, holding the hoof tightly in his hand. The bull struggled frantically to escape, leaping all around. It finally managed to get away—but had to leave its hoof in Polydamas's hand!

Most ancient bronze statues were melted down centuries ago—bronze is a valuable metal, used in later ages to make armor, cannons, and other weapons—so this statue is especially precious. It shows a young man who has just won a chariot race, still holding his reins. You might think that the horses would do all the work, but the sweat has plastered his hair down to his head, with only a few curls poking out under his headband. His mouth is slightly open as though he is panting from the effort of controlling the racing animals.

A boxer named Melankomas supposedly held his arms up in the air for two straight days to strengthen them. Try that for an hour and you'll see how hard it is!

The people who reported these superhuman feats weren't the only ones who were crazy about the games held at Olympia and other sites. In fact, the competitions were so popular that they continued long after the Greek states had been incorporated into larger units, first into Macedonian monarchies and then into the Roman Empire. In 394 CE, the Christian Roman Emperor Theodosius declared that they had to stop, since the Games were in honor of pagan deities and included prayers and sacrifices.

Although the Games were popular, they had problems, too. Sometimes the athletes found ways to cheat. Wrestlers would secretly oil their bodies so that they could slip out of their opponents' grasps. People eager to win a bet sometimes bribed an athlete to lose.

The officials wanted to make sure that the outcomes of the competitions were as honest as possible, so they declared that anyone caught cheating would be punished. Sometimes cheaters were whipped and sometimes they had to pay a fine. The sides of the stadium were lined with statues bought with their fines.

The athletes at Olympia were not paid to compete. In some other competitions, however, prizes were so valuable that they might as well have been salaries. When the judges at the Isthmian Games, for example, awarded a winner a huge jar of olive oil that was too large to carry home, surely the officials knew that the athlete would divide it up into smaller jars and sell it at a great price. Some winners would be awarded free meals at their home cities' expense for the rest of their lives. Occasionally, an athlete would play for a *polis* other than his hometown to get a better deal. Others would receive a cash prize that would pay a laborer's salary for five years. Some didn't make out as well. The winner at the Nemean Games received only a crown of celery.

All the Greek states were supposed to declare a truce during the month that the games were going on, and they took the oath: "May the world be delivered from crime and

Oh, Lighten Up– It's Only a Game!

Not everybody was crazy about sports and athletes. The playwright Euripides got especially cranky about it. He must have been one of those kids who was always chosen last for a team, because he said in a fragment of a lost play:

"*Of the thousands of evils which exist in Greece there is no greater evil than the race of athletes. In the first place, they are incapable of living, or of learning to live, properly. . . . They glisten and gleam like statues of the polis itself when they are in their prime, but when bitter old age comes upon them they are like tattered and threadbare old rugs. For this I blame the custom of the Greeks who assemble to watch athletes and thus honor useless pleasures in order to have an excuse for a feast. What man has ever defended the city or his fathers by winning a crown for wrestling well or running fast or throwing a diskos far or planting an uppercut on the jaw of an opponent?*"

THE OLYMPICS
LIVE ON

The first of the modern
Olympics took place in
Athens. About 300 athletes
from 13 countries partici-
pated. At first, athletes had
to pay their own way to
the Games, but soon coun-
tries were funding their
contestants' efforts.

Imagine an ancient
Greek athlete, naked,
sweating, competing in
sports designed to show
raw strength and speed.
Now imagine him (cleaned
up and dressed) sitting in
the stands in Athens in
2004. What would he
think of the bright modern
uniforms, of sports such as
gymnastics and synchro-
nized swimming, and of
women competing?

Perhaps he would be
shocked. But it's equally
possible that he would be
thrilled, recognizing that
under all the changes, the
spirit of competition and
the joy of performing well
are still there.

killing and freed from the clash of arms." But this peace was
broken several times. Once an army even ran through the
stadium during a wrestling match.

But still, the idea of athletes competing in difficult
events for the pure love of it was appealing to people in
more recent times. It matched many people's image of what
the ancient Greeks were like. In 1894, a Greek man named
Dimitrios Vikelas and a French aristocrat, Baron Pierre de
Coubertin, formed a committee to revive the Olympic Games.
They hoped that the glorious competition among amateur
athletes would rekindle the spirit of ancient Greece.

*Athletes from 13 countries participate in the opening ceremony of the first
modern Olympic Games in Athens in 1896. Fittingly, a Greek shepherd,
Spiridon Louis, won the marathon, the most popular event at that time.*

CHAPTER 19

STRIVING FOR PERFECTION
THE VISUAL ARTS

The philosopher Aristotle says in his *Politics* that "Art completes what nature leaves unfinished." If nature doesn't take something to its perfect conclusion, who does? A human. Art is something that is made better by humans.

But by this definition, anything well built—a machine or a brick or a bathtub—is a work of art. Some people today would agree with that, but probably the Greeks wouldn't have. Aristotle also said that art reflects an inward reality, not just the outside appearance of an object or person. Most machines or bricks or bathtubs don't have an inward reality in the way that something living does. For Aristotle, a work of art has to have meaning, and usually represents a person.

One of the most important aspects of a person, to the Greek way of thinking, was humanity's relationship with the gods. Making something beautiful for a religious reason was one way of worshiping. So it's not surprising that from the beginning, way back in the Minoan age, art was used to represent the gods and to make offerings to them. A statuette like a woman holding snakes might have helped worshipers picture the deity to whom they were praying.

The bull was very important in the religion of the Minoans. A beautiful drinking-cup in the shape of a bull's head is one of the treasures of Minoan art. This cup is obviously not very practical. It would be hard to hold and even

❝ Aristotle, *Politics*, mid-fourth century BCE

❝ Minoan drinking cup, about 1700–1400 BCE

This rhyton, or drinking cup, was sipped from its neck end. Many rhytons had pointed bases and rested on a table with holes that supported them. It is hard to imagine the shape of a hole that could support this bull's head. It was probably rarely used or used only in a ritual where it would be passed from hand to hand.

A MATTER OF TASTE

The islands in the Aegean Sea known as the Cyclades were under Minoan control, but their art was very much their own. Most of it shows oddly geometric, featureless people. Why didn't the artists show facial features? Maybe the eyes and mouth were painted on. Or maybe the stone was too hard for their crude tools. But maybe it was a conscious stylistic choice and the artists preferred their sculptures to have few details.

Plato, *Theaetetus*, early fourth century BCE

harder to drink from. You would have to hold it upside down, so it would look like you were drinking from its neck. And how would you put it down when you were through? It must have been used in some religious ceremony, perhaps one where people would take turns drinking wine from it and passing it around to one another.

The later civilization of the Mycenaeans worshiped gods, too, but they were also eager to show off how powerful they were. An ancient traveler entering the great city of Mycenae would have to wind up a hill, which would make his curiosity about the citadel get stronger as his legs got tired. And to enter, he would have to pass through a huge gate. "How could anyone move those huge stones?" he might wonder, and then he would look up.

Directly overhead, two huge stone lions stood over the arch of the gate. Their heads have been destroyed over the millennia, but they must have looked ferocious. If the traveler had forgotten, in his long climb, that he was about to enter the domain of a very powerful king, these lions would make the memory come back in a hurry.

But as we know, while the Greeks revered their gods deeply, they were also very human-centered. One of the most quoted statements ever made by a Greek is the philosopher Protagoras's claim that "Man is the measure of all things." The human body, especially the young, athletic male body, was supposed to be the closest thing on earth to divine perfection.

The Cycladic artist sculpted this harp player using very few details but managed to convey the mood of the musician, whose hands rest lightly on his instrument as his head is thrown back in concentration.

But the idea of perfection changed. A modern viewer might think that these two statues are not made very well because they are expressionless and identical. But to the Greeks they represented perfection. These two men are the brothers Kleobis and Biton, whose mother was going to miss a religious ceremony because the oxen hadn't come back from plowing the field in time. So they hitched themselves to the cart and pulled her all the way there themselves. This was an act of such piety that their mother prayed that they would be given a great reward. That night they died in their sleep.

To the Greeks this was a reward. The boys died when they were young and healthy and beautiful. They would never face war, or illness, or old age.

Nowhere in their story does it say that they were identical twins. But these two statues, made in about 580 BCE, are identical. The ringlets in their hair are so similar that the sculptor must have used a ruler to make them exactly the same. Their poses and their faces show practically no expression. Was the sculptor just not very talented?

No, this was an expensive monument made to honor Greek ideals, and the person paying for it would be sure to hire a good artist. What the sculptor is showing here is exactly what Aristotle said an artist should show: the brothers' inner reality. If the brothers were perfect, they would *look* perfect. They would also look exactly the same as each other, because their personalities were exactly the same. Most early Greek statues of men look very similar to these, and are called *kouroi* (singular: *kouros*), which means "young man." The female version is *kore*.

As time went on, Greek artists grew dissatisfied with the calm expressions and sameness of the *kouroi*. A warrior, sculpted in about 500 BCE, is dying from a painful and bloody wound. But he looks calm, and his body is lined up so perfectly that it could be used in a geometry lesson. Each little curl of hair is lined up perfectly and he's even smiling.

However, this dying warrior from the same temple, but carved about 480 BCE, is obviously at the point of death. He's slumped over, obviously growing weaker until his arm

Kleobis and Biton, about 580 BCE

Unlike earlier Greek sculptures, the Dying Warrior *shows the painful emotions an injured warrior must have felt before his death.*

MEANWHILE IN ITALY . . .

This diver from Etruria (central Italy, about 510–500 BCE) comes from a tomb. He appears to have been pushed off the cliff—look at the person who has sneaked up behind him, hiding in the bushes. Judging from the diver's grin, though, it doesn't seem to have bothered him much.

can barely hold him up. His biceps bulge with the effort and his lip is curved in pain.

At the time when the second sculpture was made, after a long and bloody struggle, the Greeks had finally defeated their enemies the Persians. For the Greeks, art was a part of life, not something tacked on when the "important" matters of politics and earning a living got taken care of. When any part of their lives changed, the art reflected it. Artists became more interested in showing feelings, whether it was the pain of death, exhaustion after a chariot race, or the strength and pride of the Greek man, newly rediscovered in the Athenians' military victory.

Figures like the brothers were certainly perfect according to the ideas of their time, but they were hardly true representations of the kind of real heroic men who had fought at Marathon and Thermopylae. One sculptor, Polykleitos of Argos, argued in his book called the *Canon* that human perfection can be shown in mathematical terms of proportion and balance. He made his stunning statue called the Doryphoros (spear-carrier) to demonstrate his ideas.

The statue shows not only the proportions Polykleitos thought were important, but also his ideas of balance. The weight shifts several times— the man's weight is on his right foot, making his knees go to the left, then his hips push to the

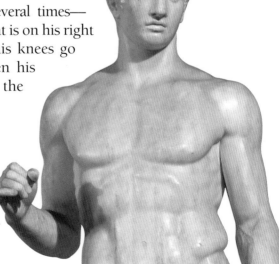

❝ Polykleitos, *Doryphoros*, fifth century BCE

The sculptor Polykleitos of Argos shows Doryphoros (spear-carrier) in a natural position, similar to how real people look, rather than in the rigid position of a stiff statue.

Classical Greek temples are rectangular with columns all around. They are classified according to the shape of columns they have: Doric (simple and undecorated), Ionic (with scroll-like design), or Corinthian (with leaf-shaped decorations). The Parthenon is a Doric temple.

❝ The Parthenon in Athens, 420 BCE

right, his shoulders left again, and finally he is looking to the right. This S-curve is not only a more natural way to stand than the rigid stance of the two brothers, but it also shows more balance—more perfection. For the Greeks of the time of Polykleitos (and for most modern viewers as well) it's also more interesting to look at than a *kouros*.

Something else happened at the end of the Persian War. The Athenians had sworn that they would never rebuild their ruined Acropolis, instead leaving its ruins as a reminder of what they had suffered at the hands of the Persians. After a while some people decided that although this would have been a nice memorial, it wasn't appropriate for the glorious city of Athens to have a pile of rocks where its public buildings used to be. So under the leader Pericles, the hilltop was transformed into one of the most spectacular set of buildings in the world. The best-known structure on the rebuilt Acropolis is the Parthenon, the temple to Athena Parthenos. Its magnificent gold and ivory statue of Athena was made by Pheidias, the most famous Athenian sculptor of the time.

Many images of children made in ancient Greece are found on funeral monuments. This little girl is saying good-bye to her pet birds.

The Greeks were very proud of their architecture. It's a form that everyone can enjoy, so it can be called the most democratic of the arts.

But wait—where were the women? Where were the children and the old people?

The sculptors of this time were interested in showing perfection. Children were certainly loved and valued by many people, but they were just potential adults, so they were not yet perfect. Old people were weaker and more liable to get ill. And in ancient Greece, women were not equal to men.

This is not to say that no Greek artists made statues of women. There were just fewer of them, and they were usually clothed. They thought that women's bodies weren't perfect the way men's were. And also, a proper woman was not supposed to go outside her house, much less show her naked body. So why go to the bother of sculpting their bodies when you could just carve a nice smooth piece of cloth, which was much easier? But as Greek women in Athens and elsewhere began getting more freedom, more statues were made of them and they were more realistic.

Several centuries later, the multicultural Hellenistic world gave artists new techniques, as different artistic traditions blended. An invention of the late fifth century BCE, the drill made it possible to make long, narrow channels in the marble. It was as though the later sculptors took everything that artists like Polykleitos had discovered and went crazy. You want smaller heads? Fine, we'll make statues with tiny heads. You want emotion? We'll give you sorrow, joy, pain!

FRIED MODELS

Greek sculptors, like modern artists, usually looked at live models while they were working. How did they get the effect of wet clothing clinging to the bodies that so many of them loved? Greece is often hot, and wet cloth would dry fast. The model would have to be hosed down at regular intervals, interrupting the process.

So a modern art historian took some linen, similar to what the Greeks wore, and dipped it in olive oil. She wrung it out and had models put it on. Sure enough, it stuck, even in the hot sun, and looked remarkably similar to the sculptures. It's possible that the ancient Greeks used this technique, despite how uncomfortable it must have been.

You like flowing cloth? Okay, here it is, with long, deep drill channels to make it impossibly rippled.

But no matter what they did, Greek artists strove for the ideal—for perfection. If you want proof of this, all you have to do is to look at the huge statues of the gods and goddesses that once adorned the triangular opening under the roof of the Parthenon. They were displayed high up in the air and they were flat against the wall of the temple. There was no way that anyone would ever see their backs.

But if you walk around a copy of one of these statues in a museum today, you will see that the back is finished as beautifully as the front. The folds of cloth, the bones and muscles, even the small wrinkles in the skin are as meticulously done as though the artist expected someone to inspect it closely. Why did they go to all this trouble with something that was never supposed to be seen?

The answer is that it didn't matter whether it was seen—it had to be perfect. The gods would see it. And the artist would see it. For a Greek sculptor, it would be falling short of the ideal to create a sculpture that was only half perfect.

Animals and other parts of the natural world were often used as decoration and were not intended to look real. The graceful curves of these dolphins would never be so similar and regularly spaced in nature—and it would be unusual to see armed soldiers riding them.

Even goddesses sometimes have trouble with their sandal straps. This Nike, or Victory, has stopped to loosen or tighten her shoe. The sculptor made expert use of the drill to carve the long, narrow folds of her robe.

CHAPTER 20

"ALL THE WORLD'S A STAGE"
GREEK DRAMA

What's your favorite kind of movie: village songs, or songs about goats? In other words, do you prefer comedies or tragedies?

"Comedy" originally meant a song sung by the village minstrel. These songs were probably funny, so our use of the word "comedy" makes sense.

About those goats, though—"tragedy" means "goat-song." Nobody's sure what goats have to do with it. There's nothing particularly tragic about a goat, after all. It's possible that goats were once sacrificed as part of a ritual at a play

The theater at Epidauros holds about 14,000 people and is still used for staging plays.

(which would certainly be tragic for the goat). So "tragedy" could be a kind of shorthand for "performance where a goat is sacrificed."

Very few Greek comedies are left for us to read today. Most of the surviving comedies are by one playwright, Aristophanes. They're pretty wild. In his play *The Birds*, some people get fed up with Athens, so they grow wings and set up a new society in the sky, called Cloudcuckooland. Actors in *The Wasps* wear wasp costumes as they play jurors, showing that juries can sting painfully. In *Lysistrata*, women all over Greece go on strike. They seize the Acropolis and refuse to have anything to do with their husbands until the men agree to end the Peloponnesian War (some of the comedies have a serious side, too).

The comedies are mostly about current events. This might explain why people of later generations lost interest in them and stopped making copies of them (which is why so few are left). If you hear a joke about a politician of your parents' time, you'll probably wonder why anyone ever found it funny.

More tragedies than comedies remain, but only a tiny fraction of what was written. And that's a shame because even today Greek tragedies are powerful and moving. Unlike Greek comedies, the tragedies were about universal themes: love, hatred, revenge, morality, duty—these are issues that people still grapple with today.

Did you ever feel that no matter what you did, you were going to get in trouble? This kind of no-win situation was the specialty of the Greek tragedians. They managed to get their heroes and heroines into a situation where any action would be punished and lack of action would be punished.

Sometimes it was the character's own fault that he (sometimes she) wound up in this fix. Usually if the main character, called the *protagonistes*, was at fault, it would turn out to be his *hubris*—arrogant pride—that got him there. But sometimes people found themselves in a mess because human relationships are complicated. Relationships between humans and the gods could get even more complicated. Trying to do the right thing, you sometimes

Sophocles's best-known plays are based on the mythical characters King Oedipus and his loyal daughter Antigone. In the myth, Oedipus is exiled and Antigone accompanies him. Here Antigone visits the tomb of her father.

have to choose the lesser of two evils. This means that you wind up avoiding doing the worse thing, but you're still doing something bad. The problem is that it's not always easy, or even possible, to tell which is the less-bad action.

For example, in *Antigone* by Sophocles, a young woman has a tough choice to make. Her brother was involved in a rebellion against King Creon and was killed. The king is so furious at the rebels that he orders that nobody bury them.

Remaining unburied was a terrible punishment for a Greek. It meant that the dead person would never be able to go to the underworld and rest. So the religious law said firmly that people whose relatives died had to make sure that they were properly buried.

But Creon is determined to make an example of these people so that his land will remain secure. This is why he made such a harsh law.

So Antigone has to decide whether to obey the king's law or the gods' law. A further complication is that she's engaged to Haemon, the son of the king. It's a classic no-win situation.

Antigone's sister isn't as independent-minded as she is. Her sister tells her:

Sophocles, *Antigone*, about 442 BCE

> No, we must remember two things; first, we were
> Born women, and women are not to get into conflicts
> With men; and second, we are ruled by people who
> Are stronger than we are, so that we must obey in
> This, and even in worse things than this.

But Antigone isn't going to take the easy way out and let someone—either her sister or the king—make up her mind for her. She decides that the gods' law is more important, so she sprinkles dirt over her brother's body. She is captured and brought to face the king, whom she calls a tyrant. Creon declares that she must be put to death.

Even though this play is taking place in a kingdom, Sophocles and his audience lived in democratic Athens, where the people's opinion was important. Behaving like citizens of democracy, the people in the play get angry at Creon's decision. "Death?" they say. "No, she deserves a glowing golden crown!"

❝ Sophocles, *Antigone*, about 442 BCE

The king ignores the people and has Antigone locked up in a rocky chamber to starve to death. But when a prophet warns Creon that something terrible will happen to his family if he allows Antigone to die, he changes his mind and has the vault opened. Too late (otherwise, it wouldn't be a tragedy)—she has committed suicide.

Her fiancé, Haemon, commits suicide in front of his father. Haemon's mother, the queen, also commits suicide. Creon has to live out the rest of his life knowing that all this death is his fault. He is stricken with grief and guilt:

❝ Sophocles, *Antigone*, about 442 BCE

> Woe for my crimes, so senseless, so insane,
> Stubborn and deadly! See the two of us,
> A father murdering, a son the murdered one.
> My wretched notions, blind, that killed my son
> While still so young, lost to the world this day
> Not through his foolishness but through my own.

But was it really the king's fault? Or was it the rebels' fault for daring to rise against their ruler? Or Antigone's, because she didn't let her king decide the right way to behave? The chorus has the last word:

> By far the greatest part of happiness
> Is plain good sense. Right treatment of the gods
> Is all-important. Boastful words,
> Spoken by boastful people, bring no good:
> Great blows will always fall upon the proud,
> And in the end these mighty blows bring wisdom.

But who are they talking about—Creon or Antigone? Creon tried to make his law more powerful than the gods' laws. But he had a good reason: protecting his people.

Antigone had a good reason to do what she did, too: she was obeying religious laws. But she was also stubborn and ignored the fact that her brother had committed a terrible crime. Theatergoers must have had lively conversations and arguments on their way home.

Since the plots of most tragedies came from myths that the audience already knew quite well, there wasn't much suspense about how they would end. People would still get caught up in the story, though, just the way you can watch a movie about the *Titanic* and care what happens to the people in it even though you know the ship is going to sink. Similarly, the audience of Aeschylus's *The Persians* would get involved in the story even though they knew that the Greeks were going to win the war.

Both comedies and tragedies were performed at the twice-yearly festivals celebrating Dionysus, the god of the grapevine. The plays were a competition. Originally, they didn't look very much like plays as we know them today. Instead of people playing different characters, two groups of 12 men would compete against each other for singing and reciting the best play in the best way. Later, someone thought of having one actor step out from the group to make a solo speech. Since he usually was responding to the chorus, he was called a *hypokrites*, or answerer.

The tragedian Aeschylus then introduced a second character, and before you knew it, full-fledged plays as we know them today were being performed. Greek plays were still performed in a competition among playwrights, though, and they still had groups of singers. This chorus would serve as a kind of a narrator or as a voice representing public opinion, not an individual with a personality.

The regular actors didn't show their personalities very much, either. Each wore a mask. Its expression would tell the audience what kind of person the actor was portraying. The masks served other purposes, too. Since women weren't allowed to act (they probably weren't even allowed to watch the plays), the man or boy who played a female role could hide his true identity. In Aristophanes' play *The Congress-women*, the Athenian women dress up as men and take over

WHY YOU SHOULD WEAR A HAT ON THE BEACH

Supposedly, the playwright Aeschylus was walking along a beach when a seagull happened to fly overhead carrying a turtle. The hungry bird was looking for a stone where it could drop the turtle to crack its shell.

Unfortunately for the tragedian, his shiny bald head looked just like a rock, so the gull dropped the turtle on him. Both the turtle and the man died.

the assembly. But the people in the audience knew that the actors were really men playing women. So they were watching men pretending to be women pretending to be men!

Also, the mask's mouthpiece was shaped like a megaphone. Although the acoustics in Greek theaters were generally excellent, a huge number of audience could attend the performance. The actors had to speak loudly enough to be heard over the crowd and the mask would help. And on a practical note, it was rare for more than three actors to participate in a play. By putting on a different mask, an actor could play a different character.

The theater was a semicircle built on the side of a hill. Since the seats were on a slope, everyone could see the action. Behind the actors, on the straight side of the semicircle, a screen or curtain (called the *skene*, or tent) served as a backstage.

Since the plot of the play would rarely be a surprise, playwrights had to come up with different ways of keeping the audience on the edge of its seat. A trapdoor could open

A member of a Greek theater audience would have no difficulty recognizing what kind of character each actor's mask represented.

The theater of Epidauros was so well designed that spectators in all the seats could hear what was said on the stage far below them.

You're Never Too Old to Learn

Many of the speeches in Greek tragedies can stand alone as poems. Here Haemon tries to convince his father to stop being so angry at Antigone:

"There isn't any shame
* when a wise man*
Allows himself to learn more
* things.*
If you're too rigid and you
* never bend–*
Well, think of trees you've
* seen in wintry storms:*
The ones that let themselves
* be swayed this way and*
* that*
Will keep their branches,
* small as well as big;*
The ones that will not bend,
* the flood rips out,*
Down to the very root,
You bend, or else you break."

Sophocles, *Antigone*

and a god or demigod like Heracles could suddenly pop up into the action. An ingenious contraption called a *mechanē*, a kind of crane, could swing an actor (usually portraying a god) out over the stage, as though he were flying.

People loved the theater. Playwrights would compete to be chosen to supply the plays. For each festival, each of the three playwrights chosen would write three plays, sometimes with similar themes, and judges would award prizes for the best ones.

Comedies, tragedies, and musical concerts were performed over the space of several days. Beautiful songs performed by the different choruses were always part of the drama. Some people would go to all the plays, hearing actors discuss difficult ideas, provide political commentary, and shake up their ideas of right and wrong. Others would laugh themselves silly over the comedies and avoid the more serious dramas. For much of the time, theater tickets were free and people of all sorts would watch the same drama at the same time. It was really democracy in action.

CHAPTER 21

GOING TO SCHOOL
GREEK EDUCATION

People occasionally question why they're learning something. Someone might have asked you why you're reading a book about ancient Greece, for example. Maybe you told them that you found it interesting. Maybe you said that a teacher assigned it, or that you had to write a report on Greece. "But will it ever be *useful* to know about the ancient Greeks?" is often the next question.

It depends on what you mean by "useful." Education does teach skills you will later use to make a living, and that is certainly useful. But it also teaches you about what human beings are like and how we got that way. What you read in books and what you do in school can help you learn how to think and how to communicate—two skills that most people, including the Greeks, consider central to human beings. So even if your future career never depends on algebra or on knowing about the birth of democracy, learning these things can make you a more knowledgeable and interesting person.

Long before there were schools, Greek children were taught the skills and knowledge they needed for their future lives. Boys were taught to farm, to make useful things, and to be

This image on the bottom of a cup shows boys attending school. The Greeks thought education taught children to be good citizens.

soldiers. Girls learned how to farm as well, and also how to weave, sew, cook, and raise children. Children and slaves did work that was considered beneath the dignity of free adults.

Probably, in the early days of ancient Greece, in the age of the poet Homer, children who were destined to be leaders also learned poetry by heart and some basic arithmetic. Boys of the aristocracy learned how to be warriors. Future priests had to memorize many prayers and rituals. These children were probably trained by people who already had these skills, not by professional teachers. Particularly wealthy boys (and perhaps a few girls) had private teachers.

Formal schooling began after the introduction of the alphabet. Sometime in the ninth century BCE, the Greeks began using their own variety of the Phoenician alphabet. The Phoenicians were traders and merchants who lived in what is now Lebanon and some of its surrounding areas. The first Greek schools we know of were established in about 650 BCE as people began rediscovering the usefulness of a written language. Most of the schools were probably set up to teach men and boys how to read and write so that they could use this skill in their work. This is an example of education being geared toward a future career.

Education in the warrior state of Sparta was also intended to teach children a clearly practical skill. The Spartans trained their young men to be soldiers and their young women to be wives and mothers of soldiers. In addition to this training, the Spartans also had schools. In fact, they had the only public schools in Greece, paid for by the government, unlike the other *poleis* where parents paid a fee. Sparta was also the only Greek *polis* to provide education for girls.

Athenian schoolboys also learned how to be soldiers. And when democracy became the form of government in Athens, it became clear that in order to be able to participate fully in the life of the *polis*, citizens were going to have to learn how to read and write—if only to be sure that the name on the *ostrakon* was really the name of the person they wanted to get rid of. So literacy, a "useful" skill, became a prime focus of education. And although the children whose parents could afford to pay were more likely to get educated, some

WHAT HAS FOUR LEGS AND A TEACHING CERTIFICATE?

Most students probably have a teacher they find a little strange. But imagine if you walked into your classroom and instead of finding a human, you saw a centaur!

That's what happened to the great hero Achilles. Although centaurs were usually wild, violent creatures, Achilles' teacher Chiron, "the most righteous of the Centaurs," according to Homer, was wise and patient. He taught his pupil the warrior arts of hunting and weaponry, as well as music and first aid—a useful skill on the battlefield.

Athenians thought that in a true democracy, rich and poor alike should at least have the opportunity to go to school. Some historians think that by the end of the fifth century BCE, most male citizens of Athens could write enough to sign their own names and write some letters.

But literacy was far from the only goal of Athenian education. In a funeral speech, the Athenian orator Hyperides declared that "our goal in raising children is to make them courageous men." Skills such as reading, writing, simple arithmetic, and physical training were obviously important, but Athenian children were being educated to be good and courageous citizens, not just soldiers, and they studied many subjects.

School was divided into three areas: reading and writing; physical training; and music and poetry (which were the same subject, since poetry was sung). Sometimes painting

66 Hyperides, *Funeral Oration*, 322 BCE

ANCIENT COMIC BOOKS

Even if it's true that most male Athenian citizens could read, at least a little, the vast majority of the Greeks were illiterate (most women, slaves, laborers). This is one reason art was so important. Paintings and sculptures could tell the story of a myth or a historical event for people that couldn't read them.

Wrestling was not just a recreational activity. Schools were for training the complete citizen, and a male citizen might be called upon to be a soldier at any time. Strength and agility were part of every boy's education.

and drawing were also taught. The Greeks didn't see the point in learning about other cultures, so they did not have history or geography classes. They didn't study science or math either. These subjects were considered important only to a very few people, who learned them through specialized study with experts.

Students weren't expected to become professional athletes, musicians, or artists—those jobs weren't considered appropriate for upper-class men, and no profession was suitable for a well-born woman—so these classes must have been considered important for molding the students into well-rounded citizens of the state. In fact, music was so central that musical ability was looked on as proof of good schooling: The philosopher Plato says in the *Laws* that "by an uneducated man, we mean someone who completely lacks chorus training; the educated man is fully chorus-trained."

Another philosopher, Aristotle, says in his *Politics* that "no lessons or labors should be imposed on a child under the age of five," and it appears that most students started school at around age seven. Boys were accompanied to school by a household servant called a **paidagogos**, who was usually a slave or a freed slave. Once at school, the student was under the control of the teacher. But unless you've really been unlucky, you've never had a teacher like an ancient Greek teacher.

The motto of the Greek school system could have been "No pain, no gain." Old men would sometimes say that they were still terrified of their now long-dead teachers. Surely some people today would also say something similar, but it would be hard to find anyone who thought this was good. But for the Greeks, fear of the teacher was not only good—it was the only way to learn.

Some of the **schools** had just a few pupils, but there are records of some with 60 to 120 students. The boys learned a lot of poetry by heart and they would practice reciting. To learn writing, the boys would make their letters on tablets coated with wax. Papyrus, an early type of paper, was much too expensive to be used for practicing letters. Once the pupils were through with their lessons and the teacher had corrected the writing, a hot bar was passed over the tablet

66 Plato, *Laws*, early fourth century BCE

66 Aristotle, *Politics*, mid-fourth century BCE

"Pedagogy" comes from *paidagogos* which means "the art or science of teaching." A paidagogos wasn't a teacher but probably had some learning himself.

"School" comes from *schole* which originally meant "leisure." Later it came to mean "what you did in your leisure time," such as study (this is what you do in your leisure time, isn't it?), and only late in Greek history did it come to mean "school."

A Greek student practicing his writing was supposed to absorb the meaning of the words as well as to learn how to make the letters. On this tablet, the student has copied out twice what his teacher wrote: "Accept advice from a wise man."

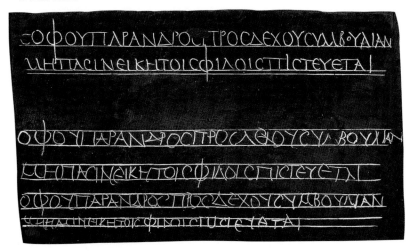

to melt the wax, and it was ready to use again. The tablet could also be used for learning math.

And moving from one group to another would be the teacher, sometimes explaining, but just as often yelling or beating someone who had misbehaved or who simply got a wrong answer.

In another building, students were tuning and playing lyres, and singing songs. Outside, other boys would be swinging blunted swords that still hurt if they hit you. Others would be tossing a discus or a javelin. Sports weren't taught to help students learn about team spirit or cooperation, or even for fun (although some boys must surely have enjoyed them). Their main purpose was training for the battlefield.

A few girls could receive a similar education, but they didn't go to school with the boys. They also probably didn't go to school as long as the boys. Girls didn't have any access at all to school past elementary education.

Very few boys went past the basics, either. Some schools were set up to provide education for future doctors and other specialists. Interested students could also get trained in rhetoric, the use of language to persuade or influence someone, or philosophy.

Books as we know them today did not exist in ancient Greece. Any text too long to fit on a tablet would be written on a scroll, which a reader would unroll with one hand, rolling up the part already read into the other hand.

Higher education got a boost in the second half of the fifth century BCE when a group of men known as the "sophists" set their minds to training future statesmen. *Sophist* originally meant "someone wise," but for these men, it meant teaching someone else to be wise.

They didn't work in schools, and in fact moved frequently from one city to another. They gave free public lectures to get people interested and then charged a fee for anyone who wanted to learn more. The sophists weren't necessarily interested in the natural world, or the world of the gods, but were definitely interested in humanity and human relations.

Some of the followers of the Sophists were young men who were hoping for a career in politics. What skills were thought most important in politics? First, how to win an argument. Then, how to make a good speech. After that, people had different ideas. Some thought a politician should have knowledge of the arts and even how to make crafts, but others thought that was a waste of time. For some, knowledge of the "four sciences" (arithmetic, geometry, astronomy, and acoustics) was essential. Some stressed that anything learned from instructors in poetry or sports was not with an eye to becoming a professional but rather for proper training in cultured citizenship.

Should you study only the subjects that will help you in a concrete, practical way in your future life? Or should you also take subjects that show you how other human beings think? What subjects would you include?

CHAPTER 22

HOW DO WE KNOW WHAT WE KNOW?

GREEK PHILOSOPHY

Wow, philosophy sounds fascinating. Old men sitting around arguing about the nature of truth and the meaning of life. They probably used words that no one today can understand and were so caught up in their thoughts that they didn't even notice the real world.

There's an element of accuracy in that. Most Greek philosophers were indeed men. Many of them were concerned with issues like the nature of truth and the meaning of life. And sometimes the right words to express their ideas didn't exist, so they made up new ones, or used already-existing words in new ways. This can sometimes make their ideas hard to understand until you learn what they intended their words to mean. But philosophy is actually something you use every day.

Imagine that it's the first day of school. The classroom looks great—you can see some interesting-looking projects on the wall and one of your best friends is sitting next to you. You didn't get the teacher you were hoping for, but your parents said this one was supposed to be really good. Then a late arrival comes rushing up between the desks and steps on the backpack that you forgot to slide under your seat. You hear a crunch and open your backpack, only to see your new calculator in three pieces. The new student apologizes. You say it doesn't really matter, that it was a cheap one, and that you have another one at home (which isn't true).

So how is this philosophy?

What is a friend? How is this person next to you a friend, and the person behind him just someone you know? Defining terms like "friendship" is part of philosophy.

What about the teacher? Why is this a good teacher? Do your friends agree that this teacher is good? Deciding what

PHILOSOPHICAL EDUCATION

Do you know someone who is called "doctor," but who isn't a physician? That person probably has an advanced university degree called a "Ph.D.," which stands for Latin words that mean "doctor of philosophy." The scholars who invented universities in the Middle Ages thought that philosophy was central to any kind of advanced learning. So anyone who claimed to be extremely well educated had to have a thorough knowledge of philosophy.

Plato, *Apology of Socrates*, 399 BCE

is a fact and what is an opinion is another part of philosophy. And when you decide that you can live with the fact that you'll have this teacher all year, you've used another aspect of philosophy: deciding what is important in life.

And those projects hanging on the wall—to you, they look exciting because your teacher last year made you do nothing but worksheets and you never got to do group projects. But to someone who had a different teacher last year, where they hatched duck eggs and raised the ducklings, a project done on paper might look boring. So some things are relative: how they seem to you depends on your own past experience. This is another part of philosophy, answering questions such as: Are all judgements relative? For instance, is it possible that it's sometimes OK to steal and sometimes it isn't? Can you prove your position?

When you told the latecomer that it didn't matter that she broke your calculator, you were lying. But you were lying to make her feel better. Does that make it OK? Deciding how to distinguish between right and wrong is a big part of philosophy.

So philosophy is connected to daily life. And the Greek philosophers were most definitely involved in the real world. Actually, philosophy arose out of curiosity about nature. The first step in the development of philosophy is trying to figure out the world.

The Greeks thought of philosophy and science as two branches of the same study. Since early Greek scientists didn't use experimentation as the definitive way to prove that something was true or false, the best way to convince someone else of your ideas was to show them how logical your thoughts were. Soon these arguments were used to explain not only the natural world, but human emotions and ideas.

"The unexamined life is not worth living." The man who said this was the earliest of the true Greek philosophers. He was the Athenian Socrates, the son of a stonemason and a midwife. At various times he was a stonemason, a politician, and a soldier. He had taken part in some of the battles of the Peloponnesian War, but he spent most of his day in the marketplace talking to whoever else happened to be there. He

It's possible that Socrates looked something like this portrait, since it was made about 399 BCE, the year he died. He is always shown as a chubby, unathletic man with a heavy beard, balding head, and snub nose.

was very good at showing people their ignorance. Once he went to a man who was supposed to be very intelligent. As he later recalled,

> I tried to show him that even though he thought of himself as wise, he was not in fact wise at all. The result was that he hated me, as did many of those who were present and heard what I said. And so, as I was leaving, I said to myself: I am wiser than this man, because neither of us really knows anything really beautiful and good, but he thinks that he does, whereas I understand that I do not. And so in that respect I am better off than he is.

66 Plato, *Apology of Socrates*, 399 BCE

There aren't many things more hurtful than to be made to feel stupid. Socrates wasn't doing this for the fun of it (although he did sometimes admit he was aware of how bad he was making other people feel), but to prove a point: that you have to think about your life and what you do, and true wisdom is hard to attain.

Paradoxically, Socrates believed that every individual knew more than he thought he knew. It was the job of every teacher to draw out the hidden knowledge and also to show people that many times, what they assume is true is actually false. He used a question-and-answer format that is now called the "Socratic method."

The playwright Aristophanes made fun of Socrates in *The Clouds*. In this play, a man trying to weasel out of a debt

{ "Paradox" comes from *paradoxos*, which means "contrary to what most people believe." Now it means something that is different from what you would logically expect.

decides to send his son to Socrates' school to learn how to argue. Socrates is presented as a silly figure who flies around in a school in the sky where other silly people talk nonsense all day long. He concerns himself with such matters as how far a flea can jump:

Aristophanes, *The Clouds*, about 423 BCE

See, he melted some wax and grabbed hold of the flea
And he dipped in its two little feet:
When the wax had cooled off, then the shoes that
   had formed
Were removed in the absence of heat,
And the size of the flea-slippers helped him to see
How the flea could perform in a meet.

People who felt stupid after conversing with Socrates must have been in stitches when they heard this mockery in the theater.

Most people thought of Socrates as just a harmless **eccentric**. But some people resented and mistrusted him. He irritated people by his questioning and he made them uncomfortable when his conversations made them question some things they had always believed in. Also, one of his pupils had been Alcibiades, an Athenian who had fought against his country. The memory of this traitor was very recent to the Athenians and some people thought that anyone who had been his teacher had to be doing something wrong.

ek + kentron =
"out of" + "center"
Someone who is eccentric is
different or odd.

So when Socrates was seventy years old, three citizens of Athens had him arrested on three charges: corrupting young people, not believing in the city's gods, and teaching about new gods. Athens had no laws protecting freedom of speech, the way many countries do today.

Socrates believed that Apollo, the god of wisdom, had commanded him to search for truth and to encourage his fellow-citizens to do the same. "Men of Athens," he said at his trial,

Socrates, at his trial, 399 BCE

If you put me to death, you will not easily find another who, to use a somewhat comical figure of speech, attaches himself to the city like a gadfly. . . .
I think the god fastened me upon the city in some

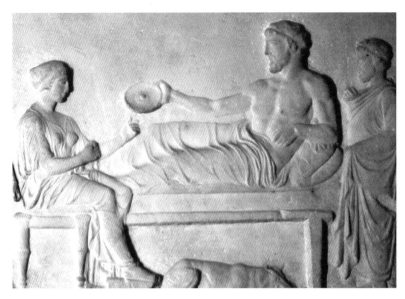

This quiet death scene doesn't correspond with the description of the death of Socrates given by Plato. According to Plato, Socrates's friends surrounded his deathbed.

such capacity as this, and I go around arousing and reproaching and seeking to persuade you, constantly alighting upon you all day long wherever I find you. Such another is not likely to come to you, gentlemen; but if you take my advice, you will spare me.

The jury of 501 Athenian citizens condemned Socrates to death by drinking hemlock, a slow-acting poison.

Some of his friends tried to convince him to escape from jail. But he said that he had always supported the laws of Athens and he wasn't about to break one of them just because he happened to disagree with it. His friends came to sit with him and they felt as sad as if they were sons whose father was about to die. Even the jailer burst into tears when he brought Socrates the cup of poison.

Socrates drank it down, and as he lay dying, his last words were to remind his friend Crito that he had promised a rooster to the god Asclepius and to ask Crito to pay that debt for him.

The Athenians came to regret what they had done to Socrates. They put up a statue in his honor, but he was still dead. Socrates was right when he warned that putting him to death was a big mistake. Thousands of years later, people who are against democracy hold up his execution as an example of the dangers of that system.

LET'S SEE, $1,000 TIMES 501 EQUALS . . .

Athenians liked large juries for two reasons: They provided a large cross-section of the citizenry and it would be so expensive to bribe them that nobody could afford it.

CHAPTER 23

TWO PHILOSOPHERS
PLATO AND ARISTOTLE

The philosopher Socrates didn't write down any of the question-and-answer sessions for which he was well known. Almost everything we know about him comes from his pupil, Plato. Plato carried on his great teacher's tradition and extended parts of it. He believed that souls were immortal and once had known all the truths. But somehow, in the process of getting born and growing up, people forget all the truths they once knew. So it is the teacher's job to help the students recall the things that they have forgotten.

Socrates rubs his chin thoughtfully as his student Plato leans against a tree during a discussion. Plato carried on the teaching tradition of Socrates and was Aristotle's teacher.

Plato carried on another practice of Socrates: he also taught young men. His best-known pupil was Aristotle. Aristotle moved to Athens just so he could study with this famous man. He was Plato's student for twenty years. Try to imagine having the same teacher for that long. Plato called him "the intellect of the school."

Aristotle and Plato had very different ideas about the nature of reality and how people could learn about it. Aristotle believed in the importance of direct observation and was interested in every branch of science. He wrote a lot about animals and was very happy when he was living by the sea because it gave him a good opportunity to observe fish.

Plato, on the other hand, based his view of the world on reason and logic. But both he and Aristotle must have been very open-minded about each others' ideas, since they stayed together at the school Plato founded, the Academy, for so long.

After Plato died, Aristotle wandered around the Greek world, teaching and doing research. King Philip of Macedon heard about this great thinker and had him come to his court to be the private teacher of his son Alexander. Alexander appreciated his teacher's interest in science and later on, as he led his armies across Asia, he ordered newly discovered animals and plants to be sent to Aristotle.

Aristotle eventually returned to Athens and started his own school, known as the Lyceum. There he assigned his pupils to write the histories of the constitutions of 158 Greek states. (The only one that survives is the one for Athens.) This is exactly the way Aristotle liked to investigate the world. You want to know how states should be run? Go out and do as much research as you can.

Plato was different. For Plato, reason (not research) was the guide. So instead of examining the governments of societies around him, he decided to use his imagination to leave the real world and come up with an ideal state.

Think about inventing your own country, with its own laws (made up by you) and its own rulers. You could decide how cities are laid out, what the schools are like, how families

SYLLOGISMS

Just because Aristotle was firmly committed to the importance of research doesn't mean that he rejected using logic to figure out how things work. One of Aristotle's main contributions to philosophy was a form of reasoning called the syllogism. His definition is: "A syllogism is an argument in which certain things being assumed, something different from the things assumed follows from necessity by the fact that they are held."

Perfectly clear, right? Maybe not. An example will help.

Tweety is a bird. All birds have feathers. Therefore Tweety must have feathers.

Or: *Paris is in France. France is in Europe. Therefore Paris is in Europe.*

So if you combine two facts that you know, you may come up with a third statement that tells you new information or confirms an idea.

In 1509 the great Italian painter Raphael united the most famous Greek philosophers in his huge painting The School of Athens. *Plato and Aristotle stand in the middle— Plato points to the heavens to symbolize his ideas about the ideal; Aristotle, with his hand stretched out, indicates the earth.*

are regulated, how children are raised, how much people get paid for different jobs, what is the right punishment for each crime—you name it, you decide it.

What would you name your country? You might name it after yourself. Or, since it exists only in your mind, you could call it "nowhere-land." An English writer in the 16th century did just that when he called his imaginary country "Utopia," from the Greek *ou,* meaning "not," and *topos,* meaning "place." Ever since then, many people have called an imaginary ideal place "a Utopia."

Plato wrote a book called the *Republic* to describe his Utopia. His ideal state has many similarities to the Athenian *polis*. It's also not surprising that a man born in Athens at the height of its powers should think of the *polis* as the best thing going. He just needed to perfect it.

The *Republic* is a long dialogue. Its main character is named Socrates, but many of the arguments and thoughts are Plato's own.

Plato discusses all sorts of ideas in the *Republic*, starting with the idea of justice. The different characters come up with different definitions of the word, and each time Socrates points out something wrong with it.

For instance, one man says that helping your friends and harming your enemies is always just. Socrates points out three flaws with this argument: First, it's sometimes hard to tell who is really your friend and who is your enemy. Second, you're going to have to live with your enemies after you harm them. In any kind of society, and especially in a democracy where people are supposed to work together, being surrounded by people who have been harmed is not as good as being surrounded by people who haven't, enemies or not. And lastly, hurting other people damages your soul.

Eventually, the speakers decide that this issue is too complex to settle. Socrates suggests that in order to understand such a huge question as the nature of justice, it would be best to imagine an ideal, perfectly just state and see how that would work. Maybe that would lead them to a better understanding of the term "justice."

Socrates finally gets general agreement that a just state is one where each individual fills the role for which nature intended him or her. And that is the basis of the ideal state described in the *Republic*.

The people of the ideal state would be divided into three classes: the Guardians (who govern), the Auxiliaries (basically, the military), and everybody else.

Who would be at the top? Plato said that people who choose not to participate in government pay a price: living under the rule of people who are worse than they. Naturally, people would prefer to live under the best rulers. But how do you figure out who those best rulers are? Not surprisingly, Plato thought philosophers would do the best job, saying,

ATLANTIS: FACT OR FICTION

The *Republic* wasn't Plato's only Utopia. He also wrote about an island-kingdom called Atlantis. This land, he says, was beautiful and prosperous. It was ruled by the descendants of Poseidon, who married its princess. The islanders dug precious metals out of the ground with ease and were surrounded by both domestic and wild animals for food. Crops grew practically on their own.

The Atlanteans ruled wisely, dividing the island into easily-governed sections. They had, says Plato, control of the whole Mediterranean area. The ten kings supplied soldiers for the army. Their cities were filled with glittering temples and beautiful public buildings.

But "in a single day and night," Plato says in *Timaeus*, "there occurred violent earthquakes and floods; . . . and the island of Atlantis . . . disappeared in the depths of the sea."

Some people think that Atlantis actually existed, but most scholars and historians look on it as another Utopia.

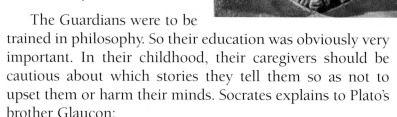

People all over the Mediterranean world were fascinated by Plato. This Roman copy of a Greek bust was found (and probably made) in Turkey.

❝ Plato, *Republic*, early fourth century BCE

There can be no hope either for our *poleis* or indeed for the human race unless either philosophers become kings in our *poleis* or the people we now call kings and rulers start taking the pursuit of philosophy seriously.

The Guardians were to be trained in philosophy. So their education was obviously very important. In their childhood, their caregivers should be cautious about which stories they tell them so as not to upset them or harm their minds. Socrates explains to Plato's brother Glaucon:

❝ Plato, *Republic*, early fourth century BCE

"Well, then," I said, "are we going to just go ahead and let our children listen to any stories their teachers may tell them, given that this means they run the risk of absorbing ideas opposite to those we think it desirable for them to have when they grow up?"

"We certainly won't allow that."

"We'll have to begin then by monitoring the people who make up stories, giving the stamp of approval to the stories we like and withholding it from the ones we reject. And we'll encourage nannies and mothers to tell the children the stories that make the cut, and we'll try to persuade them to focus on the advantages these stories bring to the soul more on those that the rubbing of the limbs brings to the body. . . . We shall never mention the battles of the giants . . . and we'll keep quiet about all those other quarrels between the gods and heroes and their friends and relations. We want them to believe us when we say that quarreling is unholy, and that never up

IT'S ALL ACADEMIC

Aristotle's Lyceum was very famous. In fact, "lyceum" became the word that some cultures use when they talk about high school. The French word for high school is *lycée* and the Italian word is *liceo*. And Plato's school was located in groves sacred to legendary Greek hero named Academus, which has given us the word "academy."

to this time have there been any quarrels between citizens. . . ."

The Guardians would, of course, investigate the nature of beauty, truth, wisdom, and the other things the philosophers found so intriguing.

Since the Guardians were not elected, but were born into their roles, obviously the ideal state in the *Republic* wasn't a democracy. It was a brand new kind of state. For one thing, Plato thought that both men and women could be Guardians. Aristotle thought that the family structure had the man at the top and that women (and slaves and children) couldn't think very clearly. He was shocked by Plato's revolutionary idea.

Plato dismissed democracy as "an agreeable kind of disorder, full of variety and handing out a sort of equality to equals and unequals alike." Some people think that Plato was so angry with the way the democratic process had killed his beloved teacher Socrates that he became anti-democratic, despite Socrates' belief that by accepting his punishment, he was supporting democracy.

Aristotle appears lost in thought, as befits a philosopher.

A Man of Strong Opinions

In his *Politics*, Aristotle was very critical of his teacher's ideas about the joint rule of men and women. He makes a point of saying that Plato and Socrates were

"*W*rong to say that excellence was the same for a woman as for a man. Excellence in men, for example, is shown in connection with ruling, but excellence in a woman is shown in connection with obeying."

CHAPTER 24

"A PESTILENT MAN"
PHILIP OF MACEDON

Beyond the borders of what many Greeks considered the "civilized" world in the fourth century BCE was the kingdom of Macedon (also called Macedonia), ruled by a strong man named Philip. One of Philip's main goals was to conquer Athens and its allies, and he succeeded.

He was able to do this because things were falling apart in Greece. The Delian League (under Athens) had been destroyed after the Peloponnesian War. The Peloponnesian League (under Sparta) didn't last much longer. So no unified force stood ready to combat Philip. In fact, some Greeks were so tired of the fighting among the various *poleis* that they thought it would be a good idea to have Greece unified, even if it was under a Macedonian. Philip looked like a good general who could beat the Persians in a fight if he had Greek armies under him. An elderly Athenian statesman named Isocrates who had lived through nearly a century of war wrote to him:

66 Isocrates, *To Philip*, 346 BCE

It is your responsibility to work for the good of the Greeks, to reign as king over the Macedonians, and to extend your power over as many as possible. For if you do these things, everyone will be grateful to you: the Greeks for your kind treatment of them; the

Philip of Macedon had a strong personality and was a ferocious fighter, who lost an eye in a battle.

Macedonians if you reign over them like a king rather than a tyrant; and people everywhere if you free them from Persian despotism and bring them under the protection of Greece.

Not everyone supported Philip. One enemy was Greece's most esteemed orator, Demosthenes. In a speech he said about Philip that "not only is he no Greek, not only is he not even related to the Greeks, but he is not even a barbarian from a place that one could take seriously. He is a pestilent man of Macedon, a land from which it has only recently become possible to buy even a decent slave."

Philip had many wives. His fourth wife, Olympias, a princess from a nearby country, was the mother of his son Alexander. Alexander's parents spared no expense in raising him. They hired tutors, including the great philosopher Aristotle, to take care of his education. The boy grew up to love Homer and even slept with copies of the *Iliad* and the *Odyssey* under his pillow. He didn't just study, though; he also learned how to fight and was taught military strategy.

When Alexander was 10 or 12 years old, his father was thinking of buying a black stallion named **Bucephalus**. But the animal was so wild that no one could control him. Alexander asked if he could try. He had

[sidebar]
Demosthenes, *Third Philippic*, 341 BCE

bous + kephalos = "ox" + "head"
Nobody knows why the horse had this odd name. Maybe his head was very large, or maybe he was as stubborn as an ox.

Demosthenes wears the traditional robes of an orator as he stands with his scroll in hand, ready to speak out against Philip.

This 15th-century illustration shows Philip of Macedon marrying his cousin, the daughter of the king of a nearby country. When Philip's chariot won a race at the Olympics a year later, the queen's name, Myrtale, was changed to Olympias to celebrate the victory.

Plutarch, *Life of Alexander*, about 100 CE

noticed that Bucephalus was afraid of his own shadow. So he whispered in the horse's ear to calm him and then took hold of his bridle and turned him around to face the sun so that the shadow was behind him where he couldn't see it. The boy then mounted the horse and rode him with no trouble.

The men were astonished, not only at Alexander's bravery, but at his intelligence. Philip said, "Look for a kingdom worthier of you, son, for Macedon is not big enough."

When Alexander was 16, his father left the country, putting his son in charge. Alexander didn't just keep things going until his father came home. When a Thracian tribe revolted, he attacked and conquered their city and set up some Macedonian colonies in their land. He named their main city Alexandropolis.

Philip's empire and his family started falling apart. First, some Greeks were afraid that the king was going to turn into a tyrant. Many men were so concerned that they abandoned Greece, sailing off to Persia to ally with that ancient enemy against this new threat. Some historians think that as many as 50,000 Greeks joined with the Persians.

And then for some reason, Philip became angry with Olympias. He accused her of adultery and declared that Alexander was not his son. He then married a Macedonian princess. At their wedding feast, the bride's uncle toasted the newlyweds, saying that he hoped that they would soon have a baby who would one day be the next Macedonian ruler.

Alexander was no fool. He knew that the uncle was implying that he, being only half Macedonian and the son of a woman who was no longer married to Philip, was not a legitimate heir to the throne. Stung by the insult, he threw his wine into the wedding guest's face. Philip, who was drunk, staggered to his feet and came at Alexander with his sword drawn, but he slipped and fell. Alexander said, "Look, friends; this is the man who wants to cross into Asia, and he can't even cross the room."

Of course, Philip was furious. Olympias and Alexander left town in a hurry.

Philip and his new wife had first a daughter, and then a son. It seemed likely that the king would declare that this boy was his rightful heir, making Alexander into a nobody. Word reached the ambitious prince that he was probably going to wind up with nothing from his father, after expecting to inherit his throne.

Meanwhile, more Greeks were flocking to the Persian side. Philip was forced to attack Persia swiftly, before the enemy forces got too huge. He sent some generals and 10,000 soldiers to make the way ready for his larger army.

Before Philip left to join his troops, he celebrated the marriage of his daughter. The bride was also Olympias's daughter and Alexander's sister, so of course they had to be invited. The wedding was a great spectacle, according to the historian Diodorus Siculus, who said in his *Library of History*:

Even at their first encounter, young Alexander knew how to control the wild stallion that he named Bucephalus. After the horse died in battle, Alexander reportedly wept during the burial.

" Diodorus Siculus, *Library of History*, first century BCE

In the procession Philip included statues of the twelve Olympian gods, crafted with the greatest skill and adorned with a dazzling display of wealth guaranteed to strike awe in the beholders. Along with these a thirteenth statue, suitable for a god, was conducted in the procession. This statue was of Philip himself, so that the Macedonian king showed himself enthroned among the Olympians. Every seat in the theater was full when Philip entered wearing a white cloak. He specifically gave orders for his bodyguard to follow him only at a distance so as to show publicly that he was protected by the good will of all the Greeks and had no need of an armed guard.

But all of a sudden one of the bodyguards darted forward and stabbed Philip between the ribs. He died instantly, and this, according to Diodorus Siculus,

> was the end of Philip, who through his own efforts had become the greatest of all kings in Europe in his day, and because of the extent of his realm had established himself as the throned companion of the Olympian gods.

The killer fled, heading for the city gates where horses awaited him. He was pursued by friends of Alexander. But he tripped on a vine and Alexander's friends captured and killed him.

The assassin was identified as Pausanias, a former friend and now enemy of the king. But did he work alone?

What was waiting for Pausanias at the gate? Horses. Plural. Not *a horse*. So someone else had to be involved and Pausanias must have believed that his co-conspirator would flee with him.

Who was that co-conspirator? Perhaps it was Alexander. Perhaps it was Olympias, ambitious for her son to become king and angry at being divorced by Philip. Or it could have been another man wanting to become king. Any of them could have bribed or convinced Pausanias to commit the murder. The mystery has never been solved.

WHAT GOES AROUND, COMES AROUND

After Philip's assassination, Olympias had his young son killed. Then she had Philip's wife executed. In fact, she murdered so many people that eventually the relatives of her victims murdered her.

CHAPTER 25

WORLDS TO CONQUER
ALEXANDER THE GREAT

❝ PLUTARCH AND ARRIAN

Alexander immediately seized control of his father's kingdom. He wasted no time in expanding his power. His first act was to put down a rebellion in the region of Thebes. When the Thebans refused to surrender, Alexander had the whole city destroyed except the temples and the house of the great poet Pindar. Six thousand people were killed and 30,000 sold into slavery. The rest of Greece was terrified at this severity and no other state threatened to rebel against Alexander's rule.

Now he was free to turn his eyes eastward, and with his army he crossed the narrow Hellespont into Asia. He quickly liberated the Greek cities that were under Persian rule there. The Persian King Darius III tried to make peace with

Alexander (far left) rides his favorite horse Bucephalus in a battle. Alexander named a city in what is now Pakistan "Bucephala" after his horse died there.

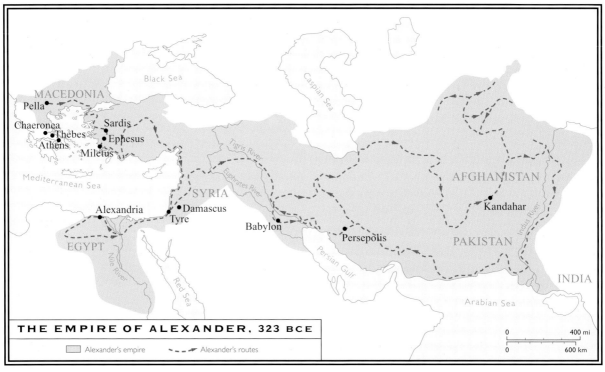

THE EMPIRE OF ALEXANDER, 323 BCE

Alexander's empire ▪▪▪▪▶ Alexander's routes

0   400 mi
0   600 km

Plutarch, *Life of Alexander,* about 100 CE

Alexander. He offered the Macedonian all the land west of the Euphrates River, a large sum of money, and his own daughter's hand in marriage. Alexander's general Parmenio said, "If I were you I would accept this offer."

Alexander replied, "So would I, if I were you!" But he was Alexander, not Parmenio, and he rejected the Persian princess, continuing his conquest of Persia. After Darius was murdered, Alexander took over his throne. He was so accustomed to living the hard life of a soldier that when he saw Darius's luxurious quarters, he supposedly said, "So this is what it means to be a king!"

Alexander told the Persians to worship him as a god. This scandalized the Greeks, who had heard many stories of disastrous vengeance by the gods on anyone who dared to compare himself with them. But Alexander said that his mother had told him that his father was really the god Apollo and not Philip of Macedon. He later said that his father was Zeus, or perhaps Amon, an Egyptian god. He also liked to compare himself with Achilles, the Greek hero of the Trojan War, and when he went to Troy he laid a wreath on the warrior's grave.

It seemed as though Alexander, even if he wasn't a god, was invincible. He was often in the front lines of an attack and, although he was wounded again and again (in his head, neck, and thigh; he also broke his leg, and his lung was once pierced by an arrow), he would heal quickly and return to fighting.

Alexander never lost a battle. He had no patience for **diplomacy**, preferring to be direct. When he arrived at the city of Gordium, he was shown a rope tied in a complicated knot. The Gordians informed him that an oracle had said that whoever untied the knot would become the ruler of all of Asia. There are two versions of what happened next. The biographer Plutarch wrote,

> Alexander, unable to figure out how to untie the knot but finding the idea of leaving it tied unbearable . . . drove his sword into it and cut the knot, exclaiming "I have undone the knot!"—at least that's what some people say. Aristobulus, though, says that he undid the knot by taking out the big pole around which it was tied.

In either case, whether he sliced the knot with his sword or pulled out the stick that it was tied on, Alexander showed he would do things his own way.

His soldiers adored him. He never asked them to do anything that he didn't do himself and was more than once the first attacker over an enemy's city wall. Once, in the desert, the soldiers were all suffering from dreadful thirst. Someone gave Alexander a helmet full of water. But he poured it out into the sand, showing them that he would not accept any special treatment.

He even looked like the Greek idea of a leader. He was handsome, with thick, curly blond hair. His eyes were interesting: one was blue-gray and the other dark brown.

Alexander moved down through modern-day Syria and invaded Egypt, where he founded the great city of Alexandria. He invaded Iraq, Iran, and Afghanistan (the

"Diplomacy" comes from *diploma*, which means "a folded paper." People with important government posts would use such papers as proof of their status. Diplomacy now means the art of dealing with people, usually representatives of another government.

“ Plutarch, *Life of Alexander*, about 100 CE

Alexander claimed that his father was not really Philip, but was either the Greek god Zeus or the Egyptian god Amon. Alexander's brother, also named Philip, decorated the exterior of the shrine Alexander had built at Karnak, Egypt, with an image of himself dressed as a pharaoh bringing a cup of drink to Amon.

SOME PEOPLE ARE NEVER SATISFIED

When Alexander crossed the Indus River, his soldiers refused to go any further. Alexander sat down and wept because there were no more worlds to conquer.

Or did he? The first time anyone mentions this story was hundreds of years after Alexander's death. Perhaps it was made up to show how ambitious he had been to rule the world.

name of the Afghan city of Kandahar is a version of "Alexander") and took over much of what is now Pakistan.

But at this point, even Alexander's loyal soldiers decided that they'd had enough. They had been traveling and fighting for ten years and now they refused to go any further. This had happened before, and Alexander had always been able to convince them to go on. But this time the soldiers were fed up. Reluctantly, Alexander agreed to return home.

But Alexander never saw his home again. On the way, he got sick in the city of Babylon after a long banquet and lots of drinking. Compared to his many injuries, this did not seem severe, but he lay ill for days. It soon became obvious that he was dying.

His followers asked him to whom he would leave his kingdom. He said, "To the strongest." This didn't give them much guidance and after he died, his empire fell apart.

Did Alexander the Great drink himself to death? Was he poisoned? Or did he contract some kind of illness? Many people adored him, but many hated him. He had great numbers of his enemies executed and shocked many Greeks by having himself worshiped as a god. Surely there were people who would have wanted to see him dead.

The people with him found it so hard to believe that he was not invincible that it took them several days to declare him dead. This must have been unpleasant in the heat of Babylon.

Alexander was buried in a solid gold coffin. His tomb was looted long ago and he was re-buried in a glass coffin. Today, no one even knows where his mummified body finally wound up. What an end for a man of whom a later Greek historian wrote, "there was no race of mankind, no city, no individual, to which his name had not reached."

66 Arrian, *The Campaigns of Alexander*, second century CE

Alexander's gold coffin was once placed inside this **sarcophagus** *decorated with scenes that show Alexander hunting and in battle.*

sarco + phagos = "flesh" + "eating" A sarcophagus is a stone coffin.

CHAPTER 26

BUT IS IT STILL GREEK?
THE HELLENISTIC WORLD

The emperor and conqueror Alexander left things in a mess by not making a clear statement about who should take over after his death. War broke out among several of his generals, each insisting that he was the one that Alexander meant by "the strongest" who should inherit his throne. These ambitious men eventually carved the empire into different parts, each setting himself up as an independent king. A general named Ptolemy had been the governor of Egypt. After Alexander's death, he had to struggle against his rivals to become the undisputed ruler of the region. He was extremely successful: his family ruled Egypt for three centuries (the last Ptolemaic ruler was Cleopatra).

After a while, the Mediterranean area became very different from the one Alexander knew. So many different civilizations were merged that the region was not Hellenic (Greek) anymore. It makes more sense to call it Hellenistic (Greek-like). Even Alexander himself was not what a purist would call "Greek." He was half Macedonian (on his father's side) and

Until Alexander proclaimed that a narrow strip of land would be his new capital, which he named Alexandria, nothing existed on that spot but a small fishing village. Today it is the second-largest city in Egypt. This 15th-century painting shows an imaginary scene of its construction.

people disagreed over whether or not Macedon was part of Greece. His mother was from Epirus, a settlement so far out on the edge of the Greek world that the historian Thucydides called its inhabitants "barbarians." And after his death, the different cultures merged and combined to such an extent that Alexander wouldn't have recognized his former empire.

This made for a change in politics. Men who used to be passionately involved in the governance of their *poleis* couldn't work up the same enthusiasm for this empire in which the individual *poleis* were no longer independent. Many people lost interest in politics and became much more involved in their families and their businesses.

Egypt's beautiful and fascinating capital, Alexandria, was home to some of the most highly-developed art, science, philosophy, and trade—everything the Hellenistic Greeks thought was important. Alexandria was a port city with two main streets, each more than 100 feet wide. They were lined with statues, colonnades, temples, and monuments. The first thing a visitor would see coming into the harbor was the palace—a whole complex of residences and offices. This huge structure reminded newcomers that government in the Hellenistic world had moved away from ordinary people and into the hands of a few powerful rulers.

Another striking Alexandrian monument was the light-house on the island of Pharos, which stood over 300 feet

NO RESPECT FOR THE DEAD

Alexander was only 25 years old when he founded his great city, named after himself. But he never lived long enough to see it flourish. He died eight years later, and his body was originally going to be buried in Memphis in Egypt. But the priest at the temple objected, saying, "Do not settle him here, but at the city he has built at Rhakotis, for wherever this body must lie the city will be uneasy, disturbed with wars and battles." So the gold and glass coffin was buried in a huge mausoleum in Alexandria. Supposedly, Ptolemy's descendant Cleopatra VII looted the gold.

THE SEVEN WONDERS OF THE ANCIENT WORLD

Ancient people loved making lists. Somebody came up with a list of the seven most amazing human-made monuments known to them (so structures like the Great Wall of China and the pyramids of Mexico are obviously not on it). The list varied somewhat, but this one is pretty standard:

The Pyramids of Egypt

The Hanging Gardens of Babylon

The Mausoleum

The Temple of Artemis at Ephesus

The Colossus of Rhodes

The Statue of Zeus by Pheidias

The Pharos of Alexandria

astro + *nomos* = "star" + "arranging" Astronomy is the study of the arrangement, motion, and makeup of heavenly bodies. Greek astronomers named their arrangements of stars after mythological figures.

tall. It guided ships into the harbor. And ships came from all over the then-known world. The different groups of people contributed their languages, customs, religions, dress, food, architecture, music, philosophy—every aspect of life. Alexandria was very different from anything the world had seen before. It was home to a dazzling mixture of people: Egyptians, Greeks, Arabs, Mesopotamians, Jews—people from all around the Mediterranean, and even further.

They mixed with one another in some parts of their lives, but not in all. At first, the Greeks discouraged marriage with the local Egyptians. The Jews lived in a separate quarter, supervised by their own magistrate. But some areas of the lives of the different groups overlapped. They traded with each other, for example. Marriage restrictions gradually relaxed, people learned each other's languages, they became interested in each other's religions. In the third century BCE, a Greek translation of the Hebrew Bible was made in Egypt.

Aside from transporting people, ships brought in books. In about 290 BCE, Ptolemy I ordered a great research institute to be built. It was named the *Mouseion* in honor of the nine Muses, the mythical patrons of art and wisdom. The government paid for about 100 scholars to work and study there. Ptolemy I also built a great library. At its height, it contained over 500,000 manuscript rolls. Travelers had to be careful if it became known that they were carrying expensive books with them. The librarian would borrow them. Then the library would keep the book and give a cheap copy to the original owner. With all these great books, Alexandria became an important center for the study of anatomy and **astronomy**.

This miniature version of the lighthouse, called the Pharos, at Alexandria is the only known representation. The lighthouse is one of the Seven Wonders of the Ancient World.

The Egyptian pharaoh at center is Ptolemy I, who was a Macedonian general. His family ruled Egypt for 300 years.

Poets, too, flourished in the Hellenistic world. Literature had declined, with no more writers like Homer or the earlier playwrights. Still, some great poets wrote works that have come down to us. Some of the most important were Callimachus and Theocritus. Theocritus was a keen observer of daily life and wrote a poem about two women, Gorgo and Praxinoa, who have moved to the city. They wander through the streets and chat about what they see. This kind of freedom for women would have been impossible in earlier days, but one of the big changes in the Hellenistic world was the living condition for women.

Gradually the restrictions on women's lives loosened. Women appeared in public and some were encouraged to write poetry and philosophy. A few women even achieved political power. Alexandria's Queen Arsinoë II appeared on coins with her husband Ptolemy II. The next queen, Berenice II, corresponded with Callimachus, and another, Stratonice, helped build the art collection on the island of Delos.

Other women were encouraged to write and even to publish their writings and appear in public. We know of some of them, including Hestiaea, a well-respected scholar. Another woman, the poet Aristodama of Smyrna, traveled through Greece giving recitals of her work.

Two schools of philosophy that didn't see any real difference between men and women, the Stoics and the Epicureans, encouraged women to attend their meetings. The two groups had the same goal: peace of mind. They reasoned that since you can't control the world around you, you might as well just not get excited about it. Then you won't wind up frustrated or disappointed. The Epicureans even thought that you shouldn't fall in love—that way you won't risk a broken heart. You shouldn't get involved in politics, either.

The Stoics also believed in staying calm, but they had a strong sense of social responsibility, so they encouraged holding public office. Although they thought that slaves and free people were equal, they never pushed for the abolition of slavery.

Science also made big leaps in this time period. Along with the mathematicians Archimedes and Euclid (whose geometrical principles are still studied today), other great scientists of the Hellenistic period included the astronomers Heraclides (who discovered that the earth revolved on its axis once a day), Aristarchus (who figured out that the earth rotated around the sun), and Hipparchus (who measured the months and seasons with amazing accuracy).

ana + tom = "up" + "cut" Scientists learn anatomy, the structure of humans and animals, by cutting them up.

Alexandria, with its great think tank of scholars at the library, attracted many scientists. The philosopher Hypatia worked and studied there. The Alexandrian **anatomist** Herophilus discovered that the brain is the center of the nervous system and that the arteries carry blood. No one had ever noticed this before; if someone is cut deeply enough to open an artery, it's hard to tell him to sit still while you see where the blood is coming from! He also studied blood pressure and figured out that taking someone's pulse often gives some clues as to disease.

Probably the most important scientist of the Hellenistic period was Eratosthenes. He was the chief librarian at Alexandria and the tutor of Ptolemy IV. He studied under Callimachus and is a good example of a philosopher-scientist. His philosophy included the then-revolutionary idea that people shouldn't be classified as either Greek or barbarian, but as either good or bad. He also wrote about Greek comedy, about how theaters worked, and about the history of philosophy.

In science, Eratosthenes was the first to use lines of latitude and longitude and proposed that if sailors went west they would eventually reach India (nobody in Europe knew that they would bump into the Americas on the way).

Greek art broke away from its traditions in this time period. Instead of depicting the "ideal" human being—the young, heroic, athletic, beautiful Greek man—artists began sculpting a greater variety of people: Africans, women, people with handicaps, old people. They showed humor: fat little children cuddling farm animals that are desperately trying to escape their attention, people getting drunk (over the last 2,000 years, some ideas about what's funny have changed), horrendously ugly people. And instead of the detached serenity of the classical statues, expressions and emotions became important.

Painted pottery became less fashionable in the Hellenistic period and wall painting was very popular. Unfortunately, hardly any of it has survived except in tiny fragments. We can get an idea of their beauty, though, from some magnificent Hellenistic mosaics that have recently been discovered.

Architecture also flourished in the Hellenistic period. Much of its popularity was due to the influence of the other cultures that were absorbed into the Greek world at this time. With a decrease in wars in the Mediterranean and with advances in navigation, people were traveling more and seeing more of the world's wonders. Ptolemy and the other Hellenistic leaders had to do something spectacular if they wanted to impress people who were used to walking next to the pyramids and other wonders of the rest of the known world. So they poured a lot of money into architecture and city planning.

Cities showed rivalry in the size of temples, a kind of "my god's better than your god" attitude. The altar of Zeus at Pergamum, in what is now Turkey, is a perfect example of this

The statue known as the Winged Victory was made around 190 BCE and found on the island of Samothrace. It is one of the most well-known Hellenistic sculptures.

66 Altar of Zeus at Pergamum, early second century BCE

German engineers moved the Altar of Zeus to Berlin in 1871.

desire to show off, and of the blending of East and West. There was no temple there, but an altar standing alone. The lack of a temple might derive from Persian influence. The historian Herodotus (who referred to the supreme god as Zeus, despite the fact that the Persians used a different name) points out in his *Histories* that the Persians

66 Herodotus, *Histories*, mid-fifth century BCE

are not allowed to built statues, temples, and altars, and in fact they accuse those who do of silliness, in my opinion because unlike the Greeks, they don't think of the gods as having human form. It is their custom to climb to the mountaintops and sacrifice to Zeus, which is the name they give to the full circle of the sky.

The sculptures on the sides of the altar showed battles between gods and giants and were supposed to represent the battles of King Attalus I. So Attalus was linking himself with the gods.

Asia, Persia, Turkey, and Greece were all represented on this huge and imposing structure. The altar of Zeus pulled much of the Hellenistic world together into one awesome monument.

THE GREEK LEGACY

Ａnd so the Greek world was transformed. A small group of people from central Italy became the next rulers of the region when they outgrew their little village on the Tiber River. They conquered Macedonian Egypt and most of the rest of the Mediterranean area, including Greece. We now call these people the Romans.

The Romans came to love Greek culture. That's fortunate for us, because it means that they passed on Greek art. The Romans copied Greek sculptures endlessly—in fact, very few Greek originals remain and most of what we call "Greek statues" are really Roman copies of Greek originals. The little we know of Greek painting (aside from vase painting) is thanks to the Romans, since their wall paintings were inspired by Greek styles. They transformed Greek

The Altar of the Fatherland in Rome, Italy, built between 1885 and 1911, was inspired by the Altar of Zeus at Pergamum. Most Romans dislike this huge bright-white building in the middle of their city and call it "the wedding cake" or "the typewriter."

FUNNY, IT DOESN'T
SOUND GREEK

The meanings of many
Greek words changed
when they entered
English. Here are some:

"Atlas" was a Titan
who supported the world.
Now, an atlas is a book of
maps because some very
early printed atlases (from
the 16th century) had an
illustration of the Titan
on the cover.

"Cosmestic" comes
from *cosmos*. This is
because in Greek, the
same word means both
order and beauty.

"Europe" is named
after the nymph Europa
who was kidnapped by
Zeus. He took the form of
a bull to visit her and she
decided to go for a ride on
him. He galloped off into
what is now called Europe
in her honor.

"Psyche" was a girl
who married the god
Eros, the god of love. Her
name means "soul," and
psychology originally
meant the study of the
soul. Now, it means "the
study of the mind."

architecture, too, by mentally taking Greek buildings apart, adding some new elements—most notably the dome and the arch—and putting them back together in a new way.

It became fashionable for wealthy Romans to send their sons to study in Greece for a year or so. These sons would come back with new Greek hair styles and with a taste for Greek literature, art, philosophy, food, architecture—if it was Greek, they loved it.

A new religion, Christianity, grew from humble beginnings in the Middle East and spread throughout the region, replacing, in most of Europe, the worship of deities such as Zeus, Hera, and their family. The Christian St. Paul was well trained in Plato and other Greek authors. He was able to bring Christian ideas to people who spoke Greek and were familiar with the way of thinking of the earlier writers.

In the 15th century, the Italians rediscovered Greek art and philosophy, and the era called the Renaissance (French for "rebirth," although classical culture had never really died, and so was not really *re*born) gave us magnificent works of art, philosophy, and literature.

We can see ancient Greek things everywhere in our lives today. Familiar names like Nike, Apollo, and worldwide events like the Olympics, near-universal symbols like the masks of comedy and tragedy—they all come from Greece. Many Greek mathematical and astronomical methods and discoveries are still in use today. But you might not be aware of the Greek origin of many other familiar things in your life.

Almost every day, someone is voting. People are elected to office, and laws and other regulations are approved or rejected. Immigrants become citizens for many reasons, one of the most important being that they want to vote. If the Greeks had not come up with the idea of democracy, where all the citizens have an equal voice in the government, who knows what political system would be running many countries today?

Before Greek was written, alphabets represented only consonants, and the reader had to guess what vowel-sound was supposed to supply the missing vowels. The Greek alphabet was the first to use symbols for vowels as well. The Romans adopted the Greek alphabet and adapted it to their own language. Most of the western world still uses that alphabet today, and many English words come from Greek.

Most people are familiar with the story of the tortoise and the hare, but not everyone knows that it was one of the many stories told by the Greek slave Aesop. The story tells us the familiar saying, "Slow and steady wins the race." Aesop also gave us the expression "sour grapes."

The universal symbol for "doctor" is the *caduceus*, originally a staff carried by Hermes. Most new physicians swear an oath of behavior modeled on the one first written by the Greek physician Hippocrates.

Look at the public buildings or old banks in your town. Do they look similar to the buildings on the Acropolis or Greek temples with tall-standing columns?

The next time you're in the store, check out the herbs and spices. Many of them come from Greece and nearby regions and were used in cooking there. Some of these herbs were also used in medicine. As people tasted and enjoyed Greek food, they started cultivating these herbs in their own homes. Examples are thyme, oregano (whose name comes from two Greek words meaning "mountain joy"), and many others.

The caduceus, a winged staff with two snakes intertwined around it, carried by Hermes, became the symbol of medicine by mistake. It originally stood for peace, and was carried by ambassadors and other people who needed to deal with people who might be hostile. But the staff looks very similar to the rod carried by the god of healing, Asclepius, and was confused with it.

According to legend, Athena, the patron deity of Athens, gave the olive tree as a gift to her city. In return, the Athenians dedicated the Parthenon to her.

You probably see many varieties of olive oil. Olive trees were exported from Greece to Italy and then all throughout the Roman Empire, and olive oil is a favorite cooking ingredient today. Grape vines also were imported from Greece into the rest of Europe.

Do you know anyone named Melissa, Nicholas, Andrew, Cassandra, Sophie, Alexander, Marissa, Jason, Christopher, Chloe, Cynthia, Gregory, George, Angela, Alexis, Catherine, or Stephanie? These and other names are Greek in origin.

If you live in the United States, your state probably has some cities with Greek names. You'll find cities named Sparta in Georgia, Illinois, Michigan, New Jersey, and Wisconsin. There are cities named Athens in Alabama, Georgia, Indiana, Louisiana, Michigan, Maine, New York, Ohio, Pennsylvania, Tennessee, Texas, West Virginia, and Wisconsin, and counties named Athens in many states.

The *polis* of Athens was so famous for its high achievements in culture that some cities boast that they are another Athens. Edinburgh, Scotland, calls itself "the Athens of the North." Nashville, Tennessee, has so many universities that it's referred to as "the Athens of the South." Nashville's symbol is its Parthenon, the world's only full-scale replica of the temple to Athena Parthenos on the Acropolis (there's another one in Germany, but it reproduces only the outside of the Greek original). The doors at the entrance are the biggest set of matching bronze doors in the world. Each one weighs seven and a half *tons!* But they are balanced so perfectly that you can push them open or shut with just one finger.

Inside the Nashville Parthenon is the largest indoor sculpture in the Western Hemisphere, a 42-foot high statue of Athena Parthenos. It's not an exact copy of the original made by Pheidias. First of all, the Greek sculpture was made of ivory, and nobody today could slaughter dozens of elephants to get the material to make a statue, even if they could afford it. Instead, Nashville's version is made of cement. This material is so strong that the artist, Alan LeQuire, decided to do without the column that originally supported Athena's outstretched hand. Pheidias needed to add it because his material wasn't strong enough for the arm to stick out far by itself, but LeQuire thought the statue looked better without it.

Also, the original was covered with one ton of gold. The gold that highlights the hair, dress, sandals, and other parts of Nashville's Athena is in such thin sheets that it took just over eight pounds of it to cover a large part of the statue.

With all these references to ancient Greece in Nashville, no wonder their football team is called the Tennessee Titans.

But even if you don't live in the Athens of the South, or the North, or the East, or the West, once you start looking, you will see evidence of ancient Greece. This great civilization has not died; it has just changed and mixed with other cultures to help produce the world we live in today.

Just like the original, Nashville's Parthenon, the world's only full-scale replica of Athens's Parthenon, houses a huge statue of Athena Parthenos. The goddess Athena is in full armor and holds the figure of Nike, the goddess of victory, in her hand.

TIMELINE

B C E

3200–1200
Greek Bronze Age

2000
Cretans build first palaces in Crete

1800
Minoans develop Linear A writing

1600
Small Greek king-
doms develop like
that of Mycenae;
shaft graves are
dug at Mycenae

1500–1450
Mycenaeans conquer
Crete

1450
Linear B syllabary
writing develops

1400–1200
Mycenae is at the height of it power

1200
According to Homer's *Iliad*, a war
occurs in Troy; Bronze Age
civilizations collapse throughout
Mediterranean; Egyptian records
report trouble made by those they
call "Sea Peoples"

1200–900
Early Dark Age; bronze gives way to iron
as iron technology develops

900–750
Late Dark Age; Greece's population
grows; trade and manufacture expand;
art of writing is recovered, but this
time as the Greek alphabet we know
today; first temples are built

776
Greeks, according to tradition, hold
their first Olympic games

753
According to legend, Rome
is established

750–490
Archaic Age

750–550
Age of colonization begins

750–700
The *polis* emerges; Homer composes
the *Iliad* and the *Odyssey* possibly
in this period

594
Solon reforms laws at Athens

560–510
Peisistratus and sons rule in Athens

525
Aeschylus is born

499–494
Ionian Greeks rebel against Persian King

498
Sardis is destroyed

496
Sophocles is born

490
Athenians defeat Persians at Battle of Marathon

489–323
Classical Age

486
Darius of Persia dies and is succeeded by Xerxes

482
Athenians ostracize Aristides

480
Persians defeat Spartans at the Thermopylae pass; King Leonidas of Sparta dies; Greeks defeat Persians at naval battle at Salamis

478
The Delian League is founded

472
Aeschylus's play *The Persians* is performed at Athens

470
Socrates is born

460–429
Pericles is the most prominent politician in Athens

460–446
Intermittent fighting occurs between Athens and Sparta

458–456
The "Long Walls" are built connecting Athens to its port Piraeus

455
Aeschylus dies

450
Aristophanes is born

446
Athens and Sparta sign the Thirty Years' Peace treaty

442
Sophocles's play *Antigone* is performed at Athens

431
Peloponnesian War breaks out

430
Plague hits Athens

429
Pericles dies

428
Plato is born

424
Thucydides is exiled

421
Peace is signed between Athens and Sparta

415
Mutilation of sacred statues at Athens; Athenians set out to attack Sicily; Alcibiades is recalled for trial and defects to Sparta

413
Athenian forces are defeated in Sicily

411
Aristophanes's *Lysistrata* is performed

408
Alcibiades is permitted to return to Athens

406
Alcibiades is deposed from generalship, possibly exiled; Sophocles dies

405
Lysander defeats Athenians at sea; 3,000 Athenians are executed

404
Athens surrenders to Sparta

399
Socrates is tried and executed

388
Aristophanes dies

387
Plato's Academy is founded

384
Aristotle is born

367–347
Aristotle studies at Plato's Academy

359
Philip becomes King of Macedon

357
Philip of Macedon marries Olympias

356
Alexander, son of Philip and Olympias is born

347
Plato dies

338
Philip of Macedon defeats Greek forces at Battle of Chaeronea

336
Philip is murdered at his daughter's wedding; Alexander becomes king

335
Thebes revolts and is destroyed by Alexander; Aristotle founds Lyceum in Athens

334
Alexander crosses over into Asia

333
Alexander cuts knot at Gordium

331
Alexander founds Alexandria in Egypt

326
Alexander campaigns in India

325
Alexander leads his troops on deadly homeward march through desert

323–30
Hellenistic Age

323
Alexander dies in Babylon at age 32

322
Aristotle dies

315
Olympias is executed

310
Zeno founds Stoic school at Athens

305–282
Ptolemy I reigns in Egypt and establishes Mouseion and Library at Alexandria

30
Cleopatra VII commits suicide after her defeat by Rome, and Egypt is incorporated into the Roman empire; all territory of former Hellenistic kingdoms falls into Roman hands

C E

330
Roman emperor Constantine founds new capital of Roman empire in Byzantium, calls it Constantinople

330–1453
Byzantine era in Greek world

394
Roman emperor Theodosius calls for end to Olympic games

1453
Turkey conquers Greece

1821–1832
Greeks rebel against Turkey; the state of modern Greece is established

1870
Heinrich Schliemann begins digging at Troy

1894
Olympic games are revived; Sir Arthur Evans begins to excavate at Knossos

1896
First modern Olympic Games are held in Athens

1953
Michael Ventris deciphers Linear B script

FURTHER READING

Entries with 󠁛󠁝 indicate primary source material.

GENERAL WORKS ON ANCIENT GREECE

Amos, H. D., and A. G. P. Lang. *These Were the Greeks*. Chester Springs, Pa.: Dufour, 1996.

Arrianus, Flavius. *The Campaigns of Alexander*, trans. Aubrey De Selincourt. New York: Viking, 1976.

Asimov, Isaac. *The Greeks: A Great Adventure*. Boston: Houghton Mifflin, 1965.

Burrell, Roy, and Peter Connolly. *Oxford First Ancient History*. New York: Oxford University Press, 1994.

Finley, Moses I., ed. *The Greek Historians: The Essence of Herodotus, Thucydides, Xenophon, Polybius*. New York: Viking, 1977.

󠁛󠁝 Herodotus. *The Histories*, trans. Walter Blanco, ed. Walter Blanco and Jennifer Roberts. New York: W. W. Norton, 1992.

Loverance, Rowena, and Tim Wood. *Ancient Greece*. New York: Viking, 1992.

Martin, Thomas. *Ancient Greece: From Prehistoric to Hellenistic Times*. New Haven, Conn.: Yale University Press, 2000.

Pearson, Anne. *Eyewitness: Ancient Greece*. New York: Dorling Kindersley, 2000.

Pomeroy, Sarah B., Stanley M. Burstein, Walter Donlan, and Jennifer Tolbert Roberts. *A Brief History of Ancient Greece: Politics, Society, and Culture*. New York: Oxford University Press, 2004.

Powell, Anton. *The Greek News: History News*. Cambridge, Mass.: Candlewick, 1996.

Solway, Andrew, and Peter Connolly. *Ancient Greece*. New York: Oxford University Press, 2001.

󠁛󠁝 Thucydides. *The Peloponnesian War*, trans. Walter Blanco, ed. Walter Blanco and Jennifer Roberts. New York: W. W. Norton, 1998.

ATLASES

Haywood, John. *World Atlas of the Past, Vol. 1: The Ancient World*. New York: Oxford University Press, 1999.

Morkot, Robert. *The Penguin Historical Atlas of Ancient Greece*. New York: Penguin, 1997.

Powell, Anton. *Ancient Greece: Cultural Atlas for Young People*. New York: Facts on File, 2003.

Schoder, Raymond V. *Wings over Hellas: Ancient Greece from the Air*. New York: Oxford University Press, 1974.

DICTIONARIES AND ENCYCLOPEDIAS

Sacks, David, and Oswyn Murray. *A Dictionary of the Ancient Greek World*. New York: Oxford University Press, 1997.

Sheehan, Sean. *Illustrated Encyclopedia of Ancient Greece*. Los Angeles: Getty Trust Publications, 2002.

BIOGRAPHY

Baker, Rosalie F., and Charles F. Baker III. *Ancient Greeks: Creating the Classical Tradition*. New York: Oxford University Press, 1997.

Cunliffe, Barry. *The Extaordinary Voyage of Pytheas the Greek*. New York: Penguin, 2003.

Fox, Robin Lane. *The Search for Alexander*. New York: Boston: Little, Brown, 1980.

Nardo, Don. *The Trial of Socrates*. San Diego, Calif.: Lucent, 1997.

[66] Plutarch. *Greek Lives: A Selection of Nine Greek Lives*, ed. Philip Stadter, trans. Robin Waterfield. New York: Oxford University Press, 1999.

ART

Buitron-Oliver, Diana. *The Greek Miracle: Classical Sculpture from the Dawn of Democracy, the Fifth Century B.C.* Washington, D.C.: National Gallery of Art, 1992.

Cook, B. F. *The Elgin Marbles.* Cambridge, Mass.: British Museum Press, 1997.

Lissarague, François. *Greek Vases: The Athenians and Their Images*, trans. Tim Allwen. New York: Riverside Book Company, 1999.

Pfrommer, Michael, Elana Towne Markus, and Marion True. *Greek Gold from Hellenistic Egypt.* J. Paul Getty Museum, 2002.

ATHENS

Joint Association of Classical Teachers. *The World of Athens: An Introduction to Classical Athenian Culture.* Cambridge, England: Cambridge University Press, 1984.

THE BRONZE AGE

Caselli, Giovanni. *In Search of Knossos: The Quest for the Minotaur's Labyrinth.* New York: Peter Bedrick, 1999.

———. *In Search of Troy: One Man's Quest for Homer's Fabled City.* New York: Peter Bedrick, 2001.

Scarre, Chris, and Rebecca Stefoff. *The Palace of Minos at Knossos.* New York: Oxford Universty Press, 2003.

BUILDINGS

Beard, Mary. *The Parthenon.* Cambridge, Mass.: Harvard University Press, 2003.

Behor, G. *Ancient Greece: The Famous Monuments, Past and Present.* Los Angeles: Getty Trust, 2000.

Nardo, Don. *Greek Temples.* New York: Franklin Watts, 2002.

DAILY LIFE

Connolly, Peter, and Hazel Dodge. *The Ancient City: Life in Classical Athens and Rome.* New York: Oxford University Press, 2000.

Ross, Stewart. *Ancient Greece: Daily Life.* New York: Peter Bedrick, 1990.

Tames, Richard. *Ancient Greek Children: People in the Past, Greece.* Oxford: Heinemann, 2002.

ETYMOLOGY

Green, Tamara. *The Greek and Latin Roots of English*, 2nd. ed. Ardsley, 1994.

Macrone, Michael. *It's Greek to Me!* New York: Gramercy Books, 1999.

HOMER

Evslin, Bernard. *The Adventures of Ulysses.* 1966. Reprint, New York: Scholastic, 1989.

Homer. *The Iliad*, trans. Robert Fagles. New York: Viking, 1990.

Homer. *The Iliad: The Story of Achilles*, trans. W.H.D. Rouse. New York: Signet Classic, 1999.

[66] Homer, *The Iliad*, trans. Richmond Lattimore. Chicago: University of Chicago Press, 1987.

Homer. *The Odyssey*, trans. Robert Fagles. New York: Viking, 1996.

[66] Homer, *The Odyssey*, trans. Robert Fitzgerald. New York: Doubleday, 1961.

Homer, *The Odyssey*, as told by Adrian Mitchell. New York: Dorling Kindersley, 2000.

Homer. *The Odyssey: The Story of Odysseus*, trans. W.H.D. Rouse. New York: Signet Classic, 1999.

Sutcliff, Rosemary, and Alan Lee. *Black Ships Before Troy: The Story of the Iliad*. New York: Delacorte Press, 1993.

MYTHOLOGY

D'Aulaire, Ingri, and Edgar Parin D'Aulaire. *D'Aulaire's Book of Greek Myths*. 1962. Reprint, Picture Yearling, 1992.

Evslin, Bernard. *Heroes, Gods, and Monsters of the Greek Myths*. New York: Four Winds Press, 1967.

———. *Monsters of Mythology*. 25 vols., most on Greek monsters. New York: Chelsea House, 1987–1991.

Graves, Robert. *Greek Gods and Heroes*. Garden City, N.Y.: Doubleday, 1960.

THE OLYMPICS

Swaddling, Judith. *The Ancient Olympic Games*, 2nd. ed. Austin: University of Texas Press, 2000.

Woff, Richard. *The Ancient Greek Olympics*. New York: Oxford University Press, 2000.

SCIENCE

Gay, Kathlyn. *Science in Ancient Greece*. New York: Franklin Watts, 1990.

SLAVERY

MacDonald, Fiona. *You Wouldn't Want to be Slave in Ancient Greece*. New York: Franklin Watts, 2002.

SPARTANS

Cartledge, Paul. *Spartans: The World of the Warrior-Heroes of Ancient Greece, from Utopia to Crisis and Collapse*. New York: Overlook, 2003.

THEATER

Ross, Stewart. *Greek Theatre*. New York: Peter Bedrick, 1999.

THE TROJAN WAR

Connolly, Peter. *The Legend of Odysseus*. New York: Oxford University Press, 1986.

Evslin, Bernard. *Greeks Bearing Gifts: The Epics of Achilles and Ulysses*. New York: Four Winds Press, 1976.

Fleischman, Paul. *Dateline: Troy*. Cambridge, Mass.: Candlewick Press, 1996.

Wood, Michael. *In Search of the Trojan War*. Berkeley: University of California Press, 1998.

WARFARE

Morrison, J. S. et al. *The Athenian Trireme: The Historical Reconstruction of an Ancient Greek Warship*. New York: Cambridge University Press, 2000.

Pressfield, Steven. *Gates of Fire: An Epic Novel of the Battle of Thermopylae*. Garden City, N.Y.: Doubleday, 1998.

WOMEN

Llewellyn-Jones, Lloyd. *Women's Dress in the Ancient World*. London: Classical Press of Wales, 2002.

MacDonald, Fiona. *Women in Ancient Greece*. New York: Peter Bedrick, 1999.

Middleton, Haydn. *Ancient Greek Women*. Oxford: Heinemann, 2002.

Nardo, Don. *Women of Ancient Greece*. San Diego, Calif.: Lucent, 2000.

Reeder, Ellen, and the Dallas Museum of Art. *Pandora: Women in Classical Greece*. Princeton, N. J.: Princeton University Press, 1996.

WEBSITES

GATEWAYS

Hellenic Culture
www.culture.gr
Links to museums, monuments, and archaeological sites in Greece and provides information on cultural organizations and events.

The Internet Classics Archive
http://classics.mit.edu/
Provides more than 400 works of classical literature by 59 authors.

On-Line Survey of Audio Visual Resources for Classics
http://lilt.ilstu.edu/drjclassics2/index.shtm
Contains thorough survey of audio-visual resources for classics and links to on-line site tours of many areas of Greece.

The Perseus Digital Library
www.perseus.tufts.edu/
Compiles works of classical literature and art and various aspects of daily life.

WEBSITES

A Quick Tour of the Athenian Acropolis
www.lfc.edu/academics/greece/AcropTour.html
Provides a tour of the Acropolis and the Parthenon with images, descriptions, and drawings.

Aesop's Fables On-Line Collection
www.aesopfables.com/
Contains texts of fables of the Greek slave Aesop.

Alexandria: The Submerged Royal Quarters
www.underwaterdiscovery.org/english/projects/alexandria/
Provides detailed reports on diving excavations of the submerged royal palace of Alexandria.

Hellenic Alexandria
www.greece.org/alexandria/
Features information on the city at various times, as well as a biography of Alexandria.

A Digital Archive of Architecture
www.bc.edu/bc_org/avp/cas/fnart/arch/greek_arch.html
Shows Greek architectural elements and provides examples.

Athenian Daily Life
http://depthome.brooklyn.cuny.edu/classics/dunkle/athnlife/index.htm
Contains links to pages about different aspects of Athenian life.

Maecenas: Images of Ancient Greece and Rome
http://wings.buffalo.edu/AandL/Maecenas/general_contents.html
This is a very full collection of images of art and architecture.

Odyssey
http://mkatz.web.wesleyan.edu/cciv110x/odyssey/
Features an index of images pertaining to Homer's *Odyssey*.

Sparta: War and Valor
www.sikyon.com/Sparta/sparta_eg.html
Shows images and information on many aspects of Spartan society.

The Ancient Greek Theatre Page
http://anarchon.tripod.com/indexGREEKTH.html
Provides a history of Greek drama and dramatists, with images of Greek theaters.

INDEX

TEXT CREDITS

All texts, except where noted, have been translated or adapted from Latin or Greek by the authors.

ABBREVIATIONS

Aeschines: Adams, C. D., trans., *The Speeches of Aeschines*. Cambridge, Mass.: Harvard University Press, 1958.

Arete: Miller, Stephen, *Arete: Greek Athletics from Ancient Sources*, 2nd. ed. Berkeley: University of California Press, 1991.

Greek Lyrics: Lattimore, Richmond, *Greek Lyrics*, 2nd. ed. Chicago: University of Chicago Press, 1960.

Hippocratic Oath: http://classics.mit.edu/Hippocrates/hippoath.html.

Histories: Blanco, Walter, trans., Walter Blanco and Jennifer Roberts, eds., *Herodotus: The Histories*. New York: W.W. Norton, 1992.

Iliad: Lattimore, Richmond, trans., *The Iliad of Homer*. Chicago: University of Chicago Press, 1961.

Odyssey: Lattimore, Richmond, trans., *The Odyssey of Homer*. New York: Harper and Row, 1977.

Peloponnesian War: Blanco, Walter, trans., Walter Blanco and Jennifer Tolbert Roberts, eds., *The Peloponnesian War: A New Translation, Backgrounds, Interpretations*. New York: W.W. Norton, 1998.

Women: Fantham, Elaine, Helene Foley, Natalie Kampen, Sarah Pomeroy, and H. Alan Shapiro, *Women in the Classical World: Image and Text*. New York: Oxford University Press, 1995.

Women's Life: Lefkowitz, Mary and Maureen Fant, *Women's Life in Greece and Rome: A Source Book in Translation*. 2nd. ed. Baltimore: Johns Hopkins University Press, 1992.

Xenophon: Marchant, E. C., trans. *Xenophon, Scripta Minora*. Cambridge, Mass.: Harvard University Press, 1962.

MAIN TEXT

p. 15: Herodotus, *Histories*, 1.1.

p. 15: Thucydides, *The History of the Peloponnesian War*, 1.1 (trans. in *Peloponnesian War*, p. 4).

p. 20: Homer, *Odyssey*, 9. 39–42.

p. 21: Homer, *Odyssey*, 9. 252–5 (trans. in *Odyssey*, p. 143–44).

p. 26: Homer, *Iliad*, 1:39–41 (trans. in *Iliad*, p. 60).

p. 31: Thucydides, *The History of the Peloponnesian War*, 1. 4.

p. 41: Homer, *Iliad*, 6. 454–464 (trans. in *Iliad*, p. 165).

p. 46: Homer, *Odyssey*, 8. 62–70 (adapted in *Odyssey*, p. 122–23).

p. 47: Hesiod, *The Theogony*, ll. 22-34.

p. 48: Archilochus, untitled poem.

p. 48: Sappho (trans. in *Greek Lyrics*, Lattimore 5, p. 41).

p. 49: Sappho, untitled poem.

p. 49: Simonides, Epitaph.

p. 50: *Supplementum Epicraphicum Graecum*, 9.3, trans. Stanley Burstein, adapted.

p. 54: Homer, *Odyssey*, 1.183–4.

p. 55: Homer, *Odyssey*, 6. 8–10.

p. 56: Solon, *Elegies*, 13. 43–53.

p. 57: Solon, *Elegies*, 36. 8–15.

p. 59: Herodotus, *Histories*, 1.61, (trans. in *Histories*, p. 22).

p. 60: Popular Athenian song

p. 63: Crates, *The Beasts*, fragment.

p. 66: Xenophon, *On Household Management*, 13.11–12.

p. 66–67: Xenophon, *On Household Management*, 13. 9.

p. 67: Aristotle, *Politics*, 1260a7.

p. 69: Aristotle, *Eudemian Ethics*, 1215b24.

p. 70: Plato, *Meno*, 71.

p. 71: *Palatine Anthology*, 7.649 (trans. in *Women*, p. 166).

p. 73: Euripides, *Iphigenia Among the Taurians*, ll. 1061–62.

p. 74: Plato, *Laws*, 781C.

p. 74 (first): Homer, *Odyssey*, 1.356–359 (trans. in *Odyssey*, p. 36).

p. 74 (second): Homer, *Odyssey*, 6. 304–312 (adapted in *Odyssey*, p. 110).

p. 75: Homer, *Odyssey*, 24: 200–202, (trans. in *Odyssey*, p. 350).

p. 75 (first): Hesiod, *The Theogony*, l. 589.

p. 75 (second): Hesiod, *Works and Days*, l. 82.

p. 75 (third): Hesiod, *The Theogony*, l. 570.

p. 76: Xenophon, *Spartan Constitution*, 1. 3.

p. 77: Phintys, *On Chastity* (trans. in *Women's Life*, p. 163).

p. 83: Xenophon, *Hellenica*, 4.16.

p. 85: Plutarch, *Sayings of the Spartan Women*, *Moralia*, 241–242.

p. 86: Herodotus, *Histories*, 3.46.

p. 86: Menander, T. Kock, *Comicorum Atticorum Fragmenta*, Fragment 702.

p. 88: Herodotus, *Histories*, 1.71.

p. 92 (first): Aeschylus, *The Persians*, ll. 424–432.

p. 92 (second): Aeschylus, *The Persians*, ll. 249–252.

p. 94: Thucydides, *The History of the Peloponnesian War*, 2.37.

p. 95: Isocrates, *Antidosis*, 15.316.

p. 96: Aeschines, *Against Timarchus*, 1.27 (trans. in *Aeschines*, p. 27).

p. 98: Thucydides, *The History of the Peloponnesian War*, 2.37–39.

p. 99: Tyrtaeus, 1, 13–19 (trans. in *Greek Lyrics*, p. 14).

p. 100: Homer, *Iliad*, 5. 890–91, (trans. in *Iliad*, p. 152).

p. 102–3: Homer, *Iliad*, 14. 395–401 (trans. in *Iliad*, p. 304).

p. 103: Plutarch, *Life of Pelopidas*, 18.

p. 104: Xenophon, *Life of Agesilaus* 2.14 (trans. in *Xenophon*, p. 89).

p. 104: Euripides, *Trojan Women*, ll. 625–38.

p. 106: Plutarch, *Life of Lycurgus*, 22.2–3.

p. 110: Plutarch, *Life of Alcibiades*, 18. 2–3.

p. 110: Xenophon, *The Hellenica*, 2. 2. 3.

p. 114: Plutarch, *Life of Marcellus*, 19.4–6.

p. 115: Hippocrates, *The Oath* (trans. in *Hippocratic Oath*).

p. 118: Bacchylides, *Ode I*, 1–7.

p. 120: Athenaeus, *The Gastronomers*, 10.412F.

p. 120: Pausanias, *Description of Greece*, 6. 5.

p. 124: Plato, *Theaetetus*, 152A.

p. 132: Sophocles, *Antigone*, ll. 61–64.

p. 133 (first): Sophocles, *Antigone*, l. 699.

p. 133 (second): Sophocles, *Antigone*, ll. 1392–99.

p. 133 (third): Sophocles, *Antigone*, ll. 1348–53.

p. 139: Hyperides, *Funeral Oration*, 8.

p. 140: Plato, *Laws*, 654A–B.

p. 140: Aristotle, *Politics*, 1335b.

p. 144: Plato, *Apology of Socrates,* 38A

PICTURE CREDITS

p. 145: Plato, *Apology of Socrates,* 21C–D.

p. 146: Aristophanes, *The Clouds*, ll. 149–152.

p. 146: Plato, *Apology of Socrates,* 30D–31A.

p. 152 (first): Plato, *Republic*, 473C–D.

p. 152 (second): Plato, *Republic*, 377B–378D.

p. 154: Isocrates, *To Philip*, 154.

p. 155: Demosthenes, *Third Philippic*, 31.

p. 156: Plutarch, *Life of Alexander*, 6. 5.

p. 157 (first): Diodorus Siculus, *Library of History*, 16.92.5–16.93.3.

p. 158 (second): Diodorus Siculus, *Library of History*, 16.95.1.

p. 160: Plutarch, *Life of Alexander*, 18.2.

p. 161: Plutarch *Life of Alexander*, 18.2.

p. 163: Arrian, *The Campaigns of Alexander*, 7.30.

p. 170: Herodotus, *Histories*, 1. 131 (trans. in *Histories*, p. 48).

SIDEBARS

p. 19: Plato, *Phaedo*, 109B

p. 26: *Hymn to Poseidon.*

p. 44: Herodotus, *Histories*, 2.120.

p. 63: Aristotle, *Politics*, 1278a3 ff.

p. 66: Aesop, *The Ants and the Grasshopper.*

p. 84: Tyrtaeus, untitled poem, ll. 1–2, 13–14.

p. 107: Thucydides, *History of the Peloponnesian War*, 2.47.3–4.

p. 121: Euripides, *Autolykos*, Fragment 282 (trans. in *Arete*, p. 185).

p. 136: Sophocles, *Antigone*, 795–802.

p. 153: Aristotle, *Politics*, 1260a.

American School of Classical Studies, Corinth. Photo by I. Ioannidou and L. Bartziotou: 70; © Ancient Art & Architecture Collection Ltd: 30, 53–54, 72, 82, 93, 117, 119, 147, 166, 173; M. Andrews © Ancient Art & Architecture Collection Ltd: 79, 101; Alinari/Art Resource, NY: 55, 56, 88, 108, 153, 154, 155, 157; Cameraphoto Arte, Venice/Art Resource, NY: 164-165; Foto Marburg/Art Resource, NY: 27, 98; Giraudon/Art Resource, NY: 14; HIP/Scala/Art Resource, NY: 145; Erich Lessing/Art Resource, NY: frontispiece, 16 (top), 22, 40, 44, 58, 60, 78, 100, 115, 118, 120, 140, 152, 159, 163; Nimatallah/Art Resource, NY: 15, 38, 43, 45, 109, 123, 129 (bottom); Réunion des Musées Nationaux/Art Resource, NY: 19, 20, 21, 23, 47, 50, 62, 64, 132, 137, 142, 156, 170; Scala/Art Resource, NY: 25, 33, 42, 61, 97, 103, 125 (bottom), 126 (left), 126 (right), 148, 150; SEF/Art Resource, NY: 112 (bottom); Vanni/Art Resource, NY: 90; Werner Forman/Art Resource, NY: 16 (bottom); Archaeological Museum of Kavala: 135; Ashmolean Museum, Oxford: 37, 57; MS Gr. class. c. 76 (P), Bodleian Library, University of Oxford: 48; British Library, Wased Tablet, ADD.34186: 139; © Copyright the British Museum: 89, 110; Attributed to Douris, Greek, early 5th century BC. The Atlanta Lekythos (Funeral Oil Jug) 500-490 BC. Painted white-ground terracotta, H.31.8 cm. The Cleveland Museum of Art, 2002. Leonard C. Hanna, Jr., Fund, 1966.114; 76; Ecole Fracaise d'Archeologie, Athens, Nauplion Museum: 84; Fotofest: 136; German Architecture Institue, Athens: 68; Greek National Tourist Organization: 28, 32, 34, 52, 94, 127, 130; Image digitally reproduced with the permission of the Papyrology Collection, Harlan Hatcher Graduate Library, The University of Michigan: 112 (top); IOC/ Olympic Museum Collections: 122; The Metropolitan Museum of

ACKNOWLEDGMENTS

Art, Fletcher Fund, 1927. (27.45) Photograph © 1997 The Metropolitan Museum of Art: 128; The Metropolitan Museum of Art, Fletcher Fund, 1931. (31.11.10) Photograph © 1999 The Metropolitan Museum of Art: 75; The Metropolitan Museum of Art, Fletcher Fund, 1932. (32.11.1): 125 (top); The Metropolitan Museum of Art, Gift of Norbert Schimmel Trust, 1989. (1989.281.69) Photograph © 1992 The Metropolitan Museum of Art: 129 (top); The Metropolitan Museum of Art, Rogers Fund, 1947. (47.100.1) Photograph © 1996 The Metropolitan Museum of Art: 124; National Archaeological Museum, Athens: 104; Parthenon Museum, Nashville, Tennessee (Gary Layda): 175; Pergamon Museum, Berlin: 169; Photo by Jim Steinhart of www.PlanetWare.com: 35, 39, 65, 91, 106, 171, 174; Photo © Roemer-und-Pelizaeus-Museum Hildesheim. 1883-9-8: 167; Courtesy of the Arthur M. Sackler Museum, Harvard University Art Museums, Bequest of Joseph C. Hoppin. Photo by Katya Kallsen. © 2003 President and Fellows of Harvard College: 102; Courtesy of Stuart S. Smith: 162

Thanks to Barbara Tsakirgis for her many helpful suggestions, to Daniel Solomon for his detective work, to Ronald Mellor and Amanda Podany for their sedulous editing, to Karen Fein and Nancy Toff for guiding us through this project, and to Greg Giles and Bob Lejeune for their patience and support.

JENNIFER T. ROBERTS is currently professor of Classics and History at the City College of New York and the City University of New York Graduate Center, where she teaches Greek, Latin, and Ancient History as well as courses on classical themes in film. Grants from the national Endowment from the Humanities and the American Council of Learned Societies enabled her to complete the second of two books on Athens, *Athens on Trial: The Antidemocratic Tradition in Western Thought*. She has also co-authored several textbooks about ancient Greece and western civilization. She currently serves as president of the Association of Ancient Historians and has just completed a four year term as the American Philological Association's Vice President for Outreach. She and her husband have homes in Riverdale, New York, and in the Catskill Mountains. Between them they have six grandchildren, the oldest of whom can read this book and the youngest of whom can toddle in its directions and try to eat it.

TRACY BARRETT is the author of numerous books and magazine articles for young readers. A grant from the National Endowment for the Humanities to study medieval women writers led to her award-winning young-adult novel, *Anna of Byzantium* (Random House). Her most recent publication is a middle-grade novel, *Cold in Summer* (Henry Holt Books for Young Readers). Tracy Barrett is Regional Advisor for the Midsouth with the Society of Children's Book Writers and Illustrators. She teaches courses on writing for children and on children's literature and makes presentations to students, librarians, and teachers. She is on the faculty of Vanderbilt University in Nashville, Tennessee, where she lives with her husband and two teenagers.

RONALD MELLOR, who is professor of history at UCLA, first became enthralled with ancient history as a student at Regis High School in New York City. He is the statewide faculty advisor of the California History–Social Science Project (CHSSP), which brings university faculty together with K-12 teachers at sites throughout California. In 2000, the American Historical Association awarded the CHSSP the Albert J. Beveridge Award for K-12 teaching. Professor Mellor has held fellowships from the National Endowment for the Humanities and the American Council of Learned Societies. His research has centered on ancient religion and Roman historiography. His books include *Theia Rhome: The Goddess Roma in the Greek World* (1975), *From Augustus to Nero: The First Dynasty of Imperial Rome* (1990), *Tacitus* (1993), *Tacitus: The Classical Heritage* (1995), *The Historians of Ancient Rome* (1997), and *The Roman Historians* (1999).

AMANDA PODANY is a specialist in the history of the Ancient Near East and a professor of history at California State Polytechnic University, Pomona. She has taught there since 1990 and is currently serving as the director of the university's honors program. From 1993 to 1997 she was executive director of the California History–Social Science Project, a professional development program for history–social science teachers at all grade levels. Her work in professional development for teachers has received major grants from the California Postsecondary Education Commission and the United States Department of Education. Her publications include *The Land of Hana: Kings, Chronology, and Scribal Tradition*. Professor Podany has also published numerous journal articles on ancient Near Eastern history and on approaches to teaching. She lives in Los Angeles with her husband and two children.